Goodnight Doll

A tribute to my gay brother
and his partner on their
rollercoaster journey with
prostate cancer

Dr Angélique du Toit

ISBN: 1522989161
ISBN-13: 978-1522989165

To Jan & Andy.

My most favourite
sister & brother-in-law.

Lots of love -

Angelique

xx

DEDICATION

To all cancer patients and their loved ones

CONTENTS

ACKNOWLEDGMENTS

With gratitude to everyone who supported me in writing this tribute.

INTRODUCTION

This book is about how the ordinary lives of ordinary people going about their daily business become extraordinary due to one life-changing event. In this case the diagnosis of terminal prostate cancer. The book is a tribute to two such ordinary people who coped with the journey of terminal cancer through a love that was anything *but* ordinary. It was made more extraordinary due to the fact that it played out within the complex social environment of South Africa.

The two people in question are my brother Eugene and Pieter, his partner of 23 years. Neither of them are famous nor featured in the social pages of magazines or newspapers. They would walk the streets without being recognized, with the exception perhaps of my brother who had cared for thousands of patients throughout his nursing career. Yet their lives together were an inspiration to anyone who had the privilege of bearing witness to the exceptional bond that sustained them through the challenge of coping with terminal cancer.

Throughout their six-year ordeal, and everything that it entailed, Eugene had by his side the constant love and devotion of Pieter until the end when he breathed his last breath. They had a love and devotion for each other that I have not had the privilege of witnessing before, and it is because of their love for one another that I felt compelled to share their story with the world. The unwavering support Pieter gave my brother was an honor to behold. This book is therefore written as a tribute to both of them. I have no doubt that their story will act as an inspiration to anyone in a similar position, either as a patient, friend, partner or family member of someone diagnosed with terminal cancer.

The idea began to take shape in my mind during the last months of my brother's life and I put the idea to him and Pieter in a long email as I wanted their approval and blessing. Eugene was rather amused by the idea and couldn't understand why anyone would want to read about him and his mundane life, as he saw it. He would be astounded to think that his battle with cancer and the pain, heartache and, yes, also laughter he and Pieter shared would one day be a source of comfort and support to others. This book is unashamedly awash with emotions: humor, sadness, desperation, frustration, joy, hope, gratitude, plus many more. Anyone who has supported someone through, or personally experienced, the journey of coping with cancer will know that life is experienced much more intensely and, as Eugene would say, in technicolor.

I started the process of writing this book at the house my husband and I bought some years ago in the South of France. It is also where the book was eventually completed. Eugene loved receiving photos of the progress we had made with its renovation and he was so looking forward to coming out with Pieter for a visit while he could still travel. Alas, this was not to be. It was therefore symbolic to me that I started and completed this tribute in France, as it was a way of sharing that special environment with him. It took me approximately two years before I could even make a start. Writing it was an emotional journey and I cried many tears during its completion. Throughout the process I had endless 'conversations' with Eugene and I felt him close by, sitting next to me and reliving the memories of his life through the stories contributed by colleagues, friends and family.

Recalling the memories was bitter sweet as we were always incredibly close. This was a bond that remained strong between us even though I left South Africa many years ago. I am blessed to have had the loving relationship we shared throughout our lives and I have many treasured memories of the times we had together. Some of these I will share with you in the chapters to follow. It is impossible to separate Eugene and Pieter's lives from the environment in which they lived, mainly because our environment and culture play a significant part in shaping who we eventually become.

Therefore, throughout my accounts of Eugene and Pieter's lives and experiences, I will provide you with brief reflections on South Africa and the very complex cultural mosaic that makes up the 'Rainbow Nation'. I certainly do not profess to be an expert on the country and the challenges it has historically and currently faces, having left and lived in other parts of the world for the majority of my adult life. However, my reflections on the South African culture will hopefully provoke some thought and interest in you to explore beyond the popular and simplistic projections offered by the media and tour operators.

Eugene was a one off, unique in so many ways, as reflected in the tributes of everyone who knew and loved him. He was very talented and created beautiful works of art through embroidery. Just like the exquisite tapestries he created, so everyone contributing to this book has added their own stitches to form the overall work of art that reflects his vibrant and colorful personality.

I struggled for a long time to find my voice and style of writing. As an academic I am used to writing about the facts, research findings and my own challenges of the assumptions that underpin these so-called facts. Instead, I eventually decided that the best way to write the story of Eugene and Pieter was through the telling of stories that reflected the passion Eugene expressed in all areas of his life. The passion he had for his profession and his patients, his passion for art and music and, above all, the passion with which he lived and loved. That was one of the biggest lessons he taught me. If it is worth giving your energy to anything, it is worth doing so with abundant passion. As Pieter says, Eugene's joy came from deep within. He had a deep-rooted belief that life owed him nothing and that it was up to him to make the best he could of any situation, and this was also the attitude that sustained him throughout his six-year ordeal with cancer.

We are known and remembered through the stories people tell about us. These are passed down from generation to generation. As Eugene and Pieter don't have any children to pass on their stories to future generations, this book is my gift to them to ensure their story is captured and remembered. This book is also a tribute to other prostate cancer patients who so willingly shared their own stories with me during my background research on the disease.

However, my hope is that this book will provide comfort and support not only to prostate cancer sufferers, but to all cancer patients and their loved ones who will be living their own ordeal, or, as Eugene used to say, being on the rollercoaster ride.

CHAPTER ONE

In order to understand the extraordinary nature of the love and support Eugene and Pieter shared, I will introduce you to their life, surroundings and their individual personalities. My father was fond of saying that 'only the good die young' and that was certainly true of my brother Eugene, or Duimpie (pronounced Damepy), as he was affectionately known by his family and close friends.

Anyone who found themselves in his company even for only a few minutes could not resist being drawn to his enthusiasm, warmth and authentic love of people. He had the ability to make the person he was talking to feel as though they were the only person in the world he wanted to be with. He achieved this by simply giving the person his undivided attention, sincere curiosity and interest. He loved people and people loved him; young or old, man or woman, boy or girl.

Women in particular adored him as he was able to empathize with them and communicate an understanding of their feelings and daily lives and what was important to them. He often referred to himself as a 'flapping queen' and in his words that was probably the reason why he got on so well with women. Furthermore, he posed no threat and engaged with them without any hidden agendas.

He relished the company of people and he was a natural entertainer, sharing either interesting stories and anecdotes, in particular of his time as a nurse in various roles, or delighting people with his gift as a piano player. Because of his musical talents he was dubbed Liberace early on in his life. However, unlike Liberace he was not a well-paid entertainer, despite his talent. Unfortunately, he lacked the discipline and focus to practice for the hours necessary, which would undoubtedly have made him a successful performer. The hours in solitude would also have meant that he could not be engaged in conversation with others or bask in the admiration of a captive audience.

He much preferred to do his practicing in front of a live audience, whether that was only one or two people or the crowds he entertained in hotel lobbies or clubs as a student earning extra money. He happily responded to the pleas of our mother to entertain visitors with his musical prowess. With aplomb and a hint of anticipation, he would seat himself in front of the piano, pause for effect with his hands positioned just above the keyboard and then begin playing with gusto. In no time everyone was carried away by his enthusiasm for music and his ability to capture and hold the attention of an audience.

He had the knack of creating a party atmosphere wherever he played. Irrespective of the musical tastes of the audience, as our mother often said, he had the ability to 'make your feet tap' and no one could resist being drawn to his sheer love of entertaining. On my husband Laurence's first trip to South Africa he delighted our mother by dancing around the sitting room with Pieter, Duimpie's partner, during one of Duimpie's impromptu concerts. Our mother recounted this story many times at the sight of Laurence and Pieter jigging around the room to the sounds of Duimpie's piano playing. My own dutiful hours of practicing scales and classical piano pieces did nothing, therefore, to endear me to the musical tastes of our mother!

The nickname Duimpie means little thumb in Afrikaans, the dialect that evolved from the early Dutch settlers and one of the official languages of South Africa. Eugene was given this nickname by our maternal grandmother when he was born, as he was very premature weighing only two pounds (907 grams) at birth. The doctors gave him a 50:50 chance of survival as in those days survival rates for such tiny babies were still low. Our mother always told the story of how he slept in a shoebox because he was so small. This was no indication of the tall man he would eventually become. However, the nickname stayed with him until the end and I shall therefore refer to him as such throughout the book.

Being premature meant he suffered various health challenges that would have significant impacts on his life for many years to come. One potential health difficulty with premature babies is that they have a high risk of developing breathing problems because their lungs are not yet mature enough to breathe independently. This was true of Duimpie and his lungs struggled to cope. This weakness remained with him throughout adulthood and as a child he often contracted croup or other breathing difficulties. This weakness also manifested itself in other ways during his cancer treatment, which I will explain in subsequent chapters. My parents spent many sleepless nights during his early years, steaming the room with various oils to ease his breathing. He was rushed into hospital on more than one occasion, needing the support of oxygen.

A further health problem premature babies may develop is that of Retinopathy of Prematurity (ROP). There are a number of possible sight problems caused by this condition, which is linked to the excessive oxygen a premature baby is exposed to in the first weeks of their life. During pregnancy the retina, the light-sensitive lining of the eye, develops while the placenta carefully regulates oxygen. However, in a premature baby the regulation of oxygen levels is more difficult to achieve. Duimpie was identified as short sighted very early on in his life and always had to wear glasses. Given his health challenges our father was possibly overprotective, although understandably so. Duimpie would often be confined indoors during inclement weather, as being exposed to changes in temperature would often trigger a bout of chest infection. However, his poor health did nothing to dampen his enthusiasm for life, which he embraced fully.

The physical health problems he experienced extended to his struggle with academic pursuits. He was identified as severely dyslexic much later in life, and had the diagnosis and recognition of dyslexia been available when he was a child, life might have turned out very differently for him. He might have been spared the isolation and humiliation of being labeled as 'slow'. Again, dyslexia may possibly be a consequence of being a severely premature baby. One definition of dyslexia is that it is a reading disability that results in a difficulty with speed and accuracy of word decoding. Duimpie always struggled with reading in early childhood.

Research suggests that being very premature increases the risk of developing neurological impairment at an early age, resulting in various learning difficulties. Duimpie struggled to make sense of new situations and experiences through the use of words, and for him to reach understanding of anything new or different he needed to build a picture of it in his mind. He would often say that he had a *prentjie kop*, translated as a picture mind, and unless he could build a picture of the topic in question, he was unable to grasp it. This often caused him frustrations, particularly in education where his visual approach to learning was not appreciated or understood.

Duimpie's struggle with academic achievement in an educational system that valued and insisted on academic success meant he was isolated and his many other talents went unnoticed or undervalued. This was no doubt exacerbated by the value our father placed on academic prowess to the exclusion of other pursuits, with perhaps the exception of sports. This was especially the case given that his talents were of an artistic nature. The society in which we were brought up did not consider it 'manly' either to possess artistic talents or engage in artistic pursuits. Boys played rugby and did not participate in activities perceived as girlish. So many years of his life were either spent struggling to reach the high academic aspirations of our father and society while at the same time suppressing the many creative and undervalued aspects of his personality.

His struggles at school came to a head at the age of approximately 14 when the school he was attending wanted to transfer him to what was known as a 'special school'. In effect he would have been taken out of mainstream education and placed in a school that catered for children with various learning difficulties. In those days this carried with it a stigma that would certainly have had a life-changing impact on his confidence and interaction with society, not to mention any potential career aspirations. Our father flatly refused and, having just moved the family for professional reasons, he packed us up again and moved back to the town we had come from only months before, so Duimpie returned to the school where he had made better progress. Fortunately, our father's employers were understanding and supportive of his decision to put the wellbeing of his son before his own career.

What Duimpie lacked in academic distinction he made up for with his personality and exceptional artistic talents. These manifested themselves especially in the art of embroidery. As at that time it was not a talent associated with, nor celebrated, in a man, he pursued his passion in private and spent hours working on intricate pieces of embroidery. To me it was as though he was painting with a needle and thread. The techniques in some the tapestries required incredibly small stitches and he would often turn to a special magnifying glass that was attached to the freestanding frame onto which he stretched the canvas he was working on at the time. Not only did he complete a large number of tapestries ranging from small to almost life size, but he also acquired the skills to create his own designs. He would start with a blank piece of canvas and through complex stitches portray his chosen pictures and themes, in time developing his own unique style.

To him embroidery was also a form of therapy and he would come home from a challenging working day in the hospital and turn to his canvas. It was a way of letting go of the stresses and strains involved in being part of the medical profession. Furthermore, it provided him with a release from coping with the additional daily strains of life as a homosexual in a very conservative and heterosexual environment. We lived together for a number of years and we would spend many evenings together in companionable silence; Duimpie with his embroidery and me with a book. Given the unique originality and diversity of the many works of art he created over the years, Pieter and I have ensured that, once we are both gone, his creations will be donated to a suitable museum for others to enjoy.

During our earlier years there were three of us at home, two boys and me. It is fascinating how children from one family can be so vastly different from each other despite growing up with the same parental values. From the outset Duimpie could not have been more different from our elder brother, Charles, who was three years his senior. Charles was dark like our mother and of average height whereas Duimpie was fair and tall like our father. However, there the similarity with our father ended. On the other hand, Charles was a chip off the old block in every way other than his physical appearance, whereas Duimpie resembled the personality of our mother. He had inherited her love of people and, like her, relished being in the company of others. Our father would often jokingly say he would build our mother a house on top of a shopping mall so that she could be surrounded by people at all times.

Our mother's love of people was equally true of Duimpie. As soon as he could walk he would disappear in search of company, much to the horror of our mother. He would be found wandering around the neighborhood, often only in his nappy, paying visits to the neighbors and merrily chatting away in childish gibberish. Our mother received a phone call from a friend one day and was horrified to learn that he had phoned them a number of times over a period of days for a chat. At first the friend thought it was a coincidence but after this occurred on more than one occasion, she thought it best to share his antics with our mother. Upon further investigation it emerged that he was regularly phoning friends, as well as strangers, for a chat, much to the amusement of everyone given that he was only four years old.

His love of people wasn't the only thing that got him into trouble as a child. His creative disposition meant he was captivated by colors and throughout his life the endless variety and vibrancy of color found in nature was a source of great joy and inspiration. On one of his visits to a neighbor, intrigued by the striking silver color the neighbor was painting his metal fence, Duimpie decided his new school shoes would look splendid in the same sparkling color. So, when the neighbor took a break from his painting, the inspired Duimpie grabbed the opportunity to transform his new shoes from black to silver. Excitedly he ran home and proudly showed off his newly transformed shoes to our parents. Their response was not what he had anticipated! Our poor mother spent hours with various solvents to try to restore the shoes to their former color. She even ended up putting them in the oven to try to dry them out, with disastrous consequences as you can imagine.

Our father was the embodiment of what one would describe as a man's man, with very definite ideas as to the differing behaviors, roles and responsibilities of men and women within society. At approximately seven years old Duimpie challenged these values to the extreme, when with his usual enthusiasm he announced at the dinner table one evening that he wanted to take up ballet lessons. The volcanic eruption of our father left us all in no doubt that no son of his would ever take up ballet, no matter how talented he might be. In fairness to our father, as Duimpie grew to be more than six feet tall, he probably would not have had a successful career as a ballet dancer.

Unlike Charles, Duimpie was an anathema to our father, who struggled to understand his creative temperament. Our father was a formidable character who instilled both respect and fear in everyone he encountered. This was particularly the case among us children when we had something to hide or when we knew we had done something wrong. He was a living example of the impact our social environment has on the adults we will eventually become. He'd had the childhood from hell. His father left his mother when he was two years old, followed by a stepfather in the true storybook sense of the word. His stepfather despised him and the more he tried to break him, the more our father seemed to resist despite the cruelty, both physical and mental, his stepfather inflicted on him. He ran away from home at the tender age of 14 and fended for himself from that moment onwards. In order to find work, he had to lie about his age and fortunately, being a tall boy, this wasn't too difficult.

Our father spent about three years living as a lodger in various homes and hostels and after working all day he went to college at night. He was always passionate about education and believed it was the route to success and the way to a better life. When he was 17 the Second World War broke out and he volunteered to join the South African Air Force. His second love after education was flying and, despite his lowly beginnings, he finished the war as a pilot. He passed his love for flying on to our eldest brother who eventually followed in his footsteps, with consequences that would forever change the nature of our family.

CHAPTER TWO

The very difficult start our father had in life meant he was not very sympathetic to anyone who didn't share his drive and commitment to achieve. He was also determined to protect his family from the many challenges of life, particularly the girls in the family. It made him feel powerless when we faced our own obstacles and he was unable to slay the dragons on our behalf. This meant he was often overprotective and unwilling to allow us the freedom to explore life and make our own mistakes. His motivations came from a place of love and a need to protect, although he did not always know how to express his affections. His efforts would often come across as anger or criticism. It is only as an adult that we are able to have a better insight into the human frailties of our parents. Alas, one doesn't have this maturity and understanding when growing up.

There were many examples where Duimpie's artistic and effeminate temperament caused sparks between him and our father, and our poor mother was forever acting as the peacekeeper between the two of them. Being the larger than life character that he was, our father was of the opinion that one could achieve anything with determination and hard work. That included changing one's sexual orientation. He was of the firm belief that Duimpie just had to 'get a grip and sort himself out'. Our father had an unwavering belief that one had choice in every sphere of life and it dominated every aspect of how he lived and interacted with others. Understanding Duimpie, therefore, also means understanding our father.

Duimpie was the sensitive one and, despite being eight years my senior, I always felt the need to look after him and protect him from the world, which could be very cruel to a creative boy with effeminate qualities growing up in a very conservative society, dominated by overbearing masculine values. He also had a naïve openness that saw the best in everyone. Unfortunately, the motivations of others did not always reflect the good intentions with which he approached others. I was a headstrong rebel who flaunted tradition and what was expected of me, especially as a girl. As much as being homosexual was considered unacceptable in South African society at that time, strong and independent girls with minds of their own were also a social abhorrence. Girls were expected to be nice, to giggle and behave demurely, especially in public. I did not have a demure bone in my body and relished beating boys at their own games.

I was a tomboy, having grown up with two brothers, preferring to play with cars rather than with dolls. My father often despaired and exclaimed that I should have been the boy and my brother the girl. It would certainly have saved the whole family a lot of heartache. Just as Duimpie's request for ballet classes ignited the wrath of our father, so did my request for Scalextric cars. I never gave up on my ambition to own a Scalextric set and I eventually realized my dream, years later, with my first salary. When I was about six, Duimpie was tasked to go into town to run errands for our mother and after much begging she agreed that Duimpie could buy me a couple of cars for the racetrack, complete with tunnels and hills, I was in the process of building outside.

I described to Duimpie what I thought was in minute detail the size, color and model of the cars I wanted. He had either not listened or had no interest in cars, probably a combination of both, but much to my horror he returned home with two buses! I was speechless and at the same time devastated. The fantasies of racing the new cars around my makeshift racetrack disappeared in a puff of smoke. How could anyone imagine that racing buses around a racetrack could be as exciting as sleek sports cars? It was beyond comprehension. Duimpie and I often laughed about it years later and his disinterest in anything mechanical, including vehicles of any kind, persisted into adulthood. To him they were mere tools to get you from A to B and he had difficulty distinguishing one from the other, except for their colors, of course.

Like my older brother Charles, I had a love of cars, trucks, planes and motorbikes, but I learnt to ride motorcycles in secret as it would certainly have resulted in excommunication not only from the community we lived in, but also from the family fold. Girls did not ride motorbikes, as simple as that. There was no frame of reference in our society that would have made it acceptable behavior for any woman. I would have had less reaction from our community if I had said I was an alien from a galaxy far away than turning up in leathers on a motorbike. However, I did drive tractors and trucks and helped our father with his hobby of building houses, while Duimpie spent time with our mother and her friends, sharing recipes and knitting patterns. Duimpie would often tease me, with serious intent, that I might be one of the 'sisters', shorthand for suspecting that I might be gay as well. As it turned out I am not, but the ingrained expected behaviors of both sexes in our society made even Duimpie question some of my preferences.

As in the United States, going to the Road House was a very popular activity with the younger generation when we were growing up in South Africa. It was the forerunner of fast food takeaways and cafés where young people would 'hang out' and meet up with friends. Traditionally you would remain in the car, while a waiter or waitress would take your order and bring the food back on a tray that clipped onto the car window. Some also provided outdoor seating areas, something that can only be found in a country with a warm climate and guaranteed sunshine.

Duimpie and I would often go for a milkshake and a chat or stop off on our way home from ice-skating with the children of family friends, who were more or less around our own ages. Once every two months or so, we would go in their Volkswagen people carrier and spend an evening having fun at the ice rink in Johannesburg, about 40 minutes' drive from the town where we lived. The highlight of the evening was to stop off at the Road House on the way back for a hamburger. Duimpie was always the driver as he was the oldest and, at that time, the only one with a driving license.

One Saturday afternoon when I was 12 Duimpie suggested that we go for a milkshake at the Road House. I sensed that he had something to tell me. He seemed rather tense and not in his usual animated state when he was excited about having something he wanted to share with me. Duimpie could never have made a poker player, as his face was a mirror that reflected what he was thinking and feeling. We arrived, ordered our milkshakes, but instead of being the chatty Duimpie I knew, he was quiet and subdued.

Eventually I asked him whether something was bothering him and invited him to share with me whatever it was. We had no secrets from each other and knew we could share our deepest dreams and concerns without any judgment. He fidgeted around in his seat and didn't want to look directly at me. By this time I knew something was amiss. He started a sentence a few times and stopped, not knowing how to express his thoughts. This was most unusual for him as he was never lost for words or lacked the ability to share his ideas with gusto. In fact, when he was animated it would be a challenge for anyone else to get a word in edgeways. As it was so out of character, I became alarmed that something serious had happened or that he was in some kind of trouble. It was the turn of my imagination to run riot and I started asking all sorts of questions related to what I imagined might be the problem. Is he ill? Has he had trouble at work? Has he fallen out with anyone?

What eventually emerged was that he was trying to tell me that he was not like other boys and he didn't like girls much. It was the first time I had heard the word 'gay', which he used a number of times. I didn't know what it meant, but I had somehow always known he was different. I certainly didn't understand the intimate details of what it meant to be gay, but I intuitively knew it was different from the norm. When I told him that I knew, his face reflected both relief and horror. 'How do you know?!' he shouted with shock and disbelief. I couldn't offer him an answer, as I didn't know how I knew; I just did. We were always close, but this made us closer as he didn't have to pretend and be guarded with me in any way. At least here was one other person with whom he could just be himself, without wearing any masks and with no fear of rejection or retribution.

When we were growing up in South Africa all young men were conscripted into the armed forces after leaving school. Duimpie ended up with the army for his nine months' tour of duty. I am convinced the army was only too glad to see the back of him and I am sure he caused havoc on more than one occasion with his impulsive and enthusiastic ideas, which would almost certainly have challenged traditional army values. One such example took place during basic training. While out on maneuvers, Duimpie decided he had had enough of crawling around in the dirt and summarily got up and trekked across the field to the sergeant who was supervising the training to tell him so in person. Before even reaching the sergeant the deafening noise emanating from him made it abundantly clear to Duimpie that such impulsive behavior was not tolerated in the army and that he was to do exactly as he was ordered. With purple complexion the sergeant continued to bellow at the top of his voice and ordered Duimpie to get back, as he was now as dead as can be, having just walked across an area littered with imaginary minefields.

This was one of many examples where Duimpie challenged the traditions of the army. Very early on his commanding officer decided to get him out of harm's way and as far removed as possible from dangerous equipment such as guns and ammunition. This was not only for Duimpie's own safety, but the safety of others. Duimpie always had a fear of guns and weapons and he was therefore not very adept at handling them. Not an ideal aversion to have when in the military or during the subsequent emerging culture that more or less required anyone to carry a gun in South Africa for personal protection. When visiting the country for the first time, my husband was both shocked and amused to discover not only the usual signs one would expect to find on entering a building, such as 'No Food or Drink' or 'No Dogs', but also a sign never seen in England, 'No Guns'. My husband was so taken by the sign that he took photographs of it to prove its existence to friends and family back home.

The ebb and flow of acceptance or rejection of homosexuality makes for interesting research, particularly within the armed forces. Amazing, as it may seem, historically some cultures not only accepted, but also encouraged homosexual behavior among soldiers. This was particularly the case in ancient Greece and Rome. It was thought that it engendered cohesiveness and bravery among the soldiers as well as increased morale. An example of such openness was the Sacred Band of Thebes of 378

BC, a unit consisting of male lovers with a reputation for military prowess during battle. The elite Samurai class in Japan also openly encouraged the practice of same-sex love between adults and apprentices. How times have changed. Homosexual behavior in both the military and society has been criminalized in most cultures at some stage or another in their history. In medieval Europe executions of suspected homosexuals in the military were acceptable punishment until the 15th century. In more recent years gay men and women were prohibited from joining the military and interviews were held with prospective candidates to exclude those with so-called effeminate behaviors.

Harassment, discrimination and bullying of both a physical and psychological nature have always been a fact of life as a gay person and the military is no different. Very often such behavior would go unchecked by commanders, turning a blind eye to any covert abuse. As a gay man, Duimpie was no different and had to deal with his own experiences of abuse. Fortunately for him, he had an understanding commanding officer and he ended up in the medical corps, which was probably the best thing they could have done for him. His nurturing nature found expression in the nursing and caring of others. This experience shaped the direction his career would take once he left the army. Upon leaving, he enrolled in one of the large teaching hospitals in Pretoria, the capital city of South Africa, to begin a career in nursing. It was the perfect and most natural habitat for him and he thrived. He had found his vocation, one that would last many years, until the end of apartheid brought about changes that he perceived as an insult to the nursing values to which he was so committed.

Duimpie spent most of his formative and early adult years desperately trying to live up to the expectations of our father and society at great personal and psychological cost. Yet, what Duimpie lacked in academic ability he made up for in perseverance; a trait we have all inherited from our father. At the end of his three years of nurse training he had to sit his final exams which would determine whether he would become a fully qualified sister, a term applying to both men and women. Once qualified he would then be able to pursue any further specialist training he was interested in. Time after time he was called into the matron's office to be told behind closed doors that he had once again failed the exams.

After his third attempt, trembling with trepidation, he responded to the summons of the hospital matron. He was hoping that on this occasion she might have wanted to congratulate him in person if he had finally passed. Timidly he knocked on her door and entered upon hearing her call 'Come!' His legs nearly gave way and I think he would have collapsed if she hadn't invited him to sit down. His heart sank into the pit of his stomach as one look on her face told him that he had once again failed. She was as sympathetic as her role would allow, but the bottom line was that this was his last chance.

He was desperate to pass and studied all the hours possible. His failures had nothing to do with his commitment, but everything to do with his dyslexia and way of learning. Unfortunately, at that time this was unknown to both himself and others and he had to deal with the humiliation of repeated failure. This was just one example of the special nature of his personality. He would pick himself up and try again. We were brought up to believe that if you failed, you may allow yourself the luxury of feeling sorry for yourself for a day or two and then you got up and carried on trying until you succeeded. It instilled in us a resilience to deal with life's challenges and so Duimpie kept on trying.

At the same time I was studying for my final matric exams, the equivalent of A levels in the UK, and we shared a caravan in the back of the family garden to study, as it was quiet and peaceful. I saw the desperation and worry written all over Duimpie's face and understood the consequences if he didn't pass. Not a religious person, I nevertheless prayed to whatever higher power there was to trade my success in exam results for his success instead as I knew just how much it meant to him. This came to pass and, as I am quite academic, no one could believe that I failed in two of my subjects. However, the payback was that Duimpie had finally, on the fourth attempt, passed his exams. Yet again, the matron called him into her office and on this occasion she was the bearer of the long awaited good tidings. The huge grin on her face left him in no doubt as to the outcome of the exams. Duimpie couldn't contain himself and yelled at the top of his voice, dancing around like someone possessed. The matron, with her fierce reputation, continued to smile broadly and allowed him to vent his joy and exuberance in the expressive way that only Duimpie could do. His depth of relief and gratitude was worth every minute of the sacrifice, if that is what it was, and given the chance I would do it all over again. I resat my exams a few weeks later, passed and went on to pursue my own career, and Duimpie could forever hold his head high having succeeded to qualify and pursue his dream of training as a psychiatric nurse.

His sexual orientation was a constant source of frustration and hurt to our father, eventually resulting in a family split that would last a number of years. On the other hand as a comfort to our father, our eldest brother Charles shared his love of flying and pursued his ambition since childhood to become a fighter pilot. It was a very proud day for our father when Charles qualified as a pilot in the South African Air Force and was presented with his wings at a special ceremony. Just as nursing was the perfect environment for Duimpie, so the air force was the perfect environment for Charles. For a while his career took the focus away from Duimpie, as our father was engrossed with his progress towards becoming a pilot. However, disaster struck, changing the family forever.

When I was about nine years old, there came the dreaded knock on the door and when our mother saw the air force chaplain on the doorstep, she collapsed. It could mean only one thing. Charles had been killed during a mock air battle exercise that morning. The family was never told exactly how it happened. My parents were as devastated as only parents can be when they have lost a son. My father was utterly heartbroken as he was very close to Charles. He often reflected afterwards that the death of Charles was his punishment for caring so much for him. It was illogical, of course, but grief does not subscribe to logic.

During his darkest, grief stricken moments he made it clear that he thought the wrong son had died. There followed many difficult years when it felt as though our family life had been torn apart. My parents were not interested in anything and my father turned to work and his hobby of building houses to avoid dealing with his pain. The result was that he was too tired to come to terms with the loss of his beloved Charles. It had a devastating impact on the rest of the family and many years would pass before the wounds were healed, although the deep scars would forever remain.

The years following the death of Charles were a very difficult time for all of us. Duimpie not only had to come to terms with losing a brother, but also had to find a way of coping with the guilt of being the surviving son; not only the son who was gay but also the wrong son. I have often mused what our family life would have been like if Charles had not been killed. Furthermore, how would he, very much a military man, have dealt with and come to terms with a brother who was gay? They were close as kids and did everything together but would that bond have been strong enough to bridge the two very different worlds they came to inhabit? Would it have taken the spotlight and possibly the heat off Duimpie? We will never know and I can only speculate.

As a result, as soon as Duimpie completed his nurse training he decided to leave South Africa and went to live and work in Windhoek, the capital of Namibia, or South West Africa as it was known at that time. It was probably good for both him and our father to have some distance between them and to allow time to begin healing the wounds left by the death of Charles. It was without a doubt one of the lowest times in Duimpie's life, attempting to come to terms with his homosexuality and dealing with the knowledge that he was not enough in the eyes of our father. His confidence and zest for life were struggling to survive. Duimpie and I regularly stayed in touch via letters and occasional phone calls but I missed him terribly. I was also worried about his wellbeing and feared he would come to harm without me there to protect him. I also felt lost without my pal and confidante with whom I could share everything. We could spend hours chatting, analyzing situations from every possible angle. Our father would often ask in puzzled amazement what we could possibly be talking about for so many hours. 'Don't the two of you ever get tired of talking?!' he would ask with mild exasperation.

In the meantime, my mother had another baby. After the loss of Charles, she felt a deep need to try to fill the void left by his death and she gave birth to my sister, Lorenzi. There was a significant age gap between us and Lorenzi, who was 20 years younger than Duimpie and 12 years younger than me. I could never make up my mind whether it was fair to Lorenzi, who virtually grew up as an only child with parents who were probably more the age of grandparents and with values to match. However, like Duimpie, she continued to live near our parents as an adult and offered our mother much support with her day-to-day care after Duimpie passed away.

CHAPTER THREE

The separation from the family was very good for Duimpie, and so was Namibia. He was always attracted to German culture and Namibia was a German colony until the end of the First World War. The German influence was therefore apparent in the country's culture and customs. As with much of Southern Africa, the country is reliant on its rich supply of mineral resources such as diamonds and gold. Namibia is sparsely populated, particularly given that a large section of the country forms part of the Namib Desert. However, Namibia has a beauty of its own. It is interesting to note that Namibia is one of the few countries that explicitly addresses issues of conservation and protects its natural resources within its constitution.

One such area is the Namib-Naukluft National Park, encompassing part of the Namib Dessert. It is the largest game park in Africa and the fourth largest in the world. Winds blowing in from the Atlantic Ocean are responsible for creating the park's towering sand dunes of burnt orange. The color, a sign of their age, develops over time as iron in the sand is oxidized. Therefore, the older the dune the brighter the color. These dunes are the tallest in the world, rising to almost 1000 feet (more than 300 meters) above the desert floor in some places. I was fascinated by Duimpie's description of a phenomenon known as the singing dunes. The sound resembles that of a low-pitch rumble and is produced by winds blowing over the dunes or by someone walking near the crest. Duimpie referred to them as the 'brom-brom dunes'.

Duimpie spent much of his spare time visiting all the attractions the country had to offer and he had many stories and photographs to share with us when he eventually returned to South Africa. He was gone for nearly four years and by then our father had to some extent grown used to the fact that Duimpie was the surviving son. He also reluctantly accepted that Duimpie would never become a copy of Charles; not even remotely so. Eventually our father persuaded him to return to South Africa and supported him to get a good post at a mining hospital owned by one of the large mining companies.

After the Second World War our father had joined the gold mining industry in South Africa. Mining has been a significant source of growth and development of the country and contributed to establishing it as one of Africa's most advanced and richest economies. It has also fuelled many of the conflicts and territorial battles in the history of the region, playing an integral part in the shaping of the region and its borders. South Africa continues to be the largest producer of many minerals such as chrome and platinum and one of the largest producers of gold in the world. Our father did very well in the mining industry and was eventually responsible for managing some of the most successful gold mines, including one of the Western Deep Level mines, listed as the deepest mine in the world at the time.

It was a very male dominated environment and one our father thought would encourage my brother to overcome what he continued to perceive as Duimpie's afflictions. It was only many years later that he would come to terms with Duimpie's sexual orientation, but until then he was going to make the most of every opportunity to attempt to influence his preferences. Our father was one of the most determined people I have ever met and it was rare for him not to achieve his intended objectives.

Duimpie was a hard worker and he became a well-respected member of the hospital staff. Personally, I was very excited to have him back and it almost felt like old times. However, it became apparent to me that he was not happy in the mining environment, which was so at odds with his effeminate, creative personality. It was very much a man's world and the only women around were those in administration and clerical roles. As part of our father's duties, heading up one of the largest mines in the world, he often had to entertain overseas visitors. Sometimes these visitors would include women and he made it abundantly clear that he did not think it an appropriate environment for women, who would merely get in the way of the men running the business.

However, given our upbringing to keep trying, Duimpie persevered in stoic tradition. He also wanted to support our father in making up for his loss of Charles and in doing so living up to the expectations of our father. It was during this time that he met Karen through a mutual friend. They became very good friends and had a lot in common. Duimpie was particularly fond of her parents and, as with everyone who met him, they adored him. My unease grew as I realized her affections for him were more than those of a friend.

It is important to briefly deviate and put into context what it meant to be a gay person during the 1960s and '70s when we were growing up. Homosexuality was defined as a mental illness during the 1920s and was treated as such by the medical profession until as late as the 1970s. For example, in many of the armed forces around the world, homosexual soldiers were often subjected to medical 'cures' to rid them of their sexual orientation. There has been a range of so-called treatments over the years aimed at changing sexual orientation from homosexual to heterosexual, aversion therapy being one such treatment. It was seen as an effective treatment of addiction and dangerous and unwanted behaviors. The so-called therapy included being given vomit-inducing drugs or electric shocks. In the case of the latter, electrodes would be attached to different parts of the body such as the genitals. Electric shocks would then be administered while the 'patient' was shown pornographic pictures of men. Similar photographs would then be shown of women but without the shock treatment. The pain was perceived as part of the cure.

The brutality and ignorance of so-called civilized society as late as the mid 1950s was starkly brought to life in the 2014 movie *The Imitation Game*, which was released at the time I was writing this book. It had a particularly strong impact on me, given the persecution of the main character, Alan Turing, due to his sexual orientation. It depicted the unimaginable treatment of another human being whose only crime was that of being homosexual. Alan Turing, with his colleagues, broke Germany's Enigma Code during the Second World War, which was reported to have shortened the war by two years, saving many millions of lives. Winston Churchill was quoted as saying that Turing had made the single biggest contribution to Allied victory in the war against Nazi Germany.

It is therefore inconceivable that the society he had done so much for would reward him with the most inhuman treatment, simply because he was a gay man. After the war Turing continued with his experiments and inventions and he went on to invent the Turing Machine, the forerunner of the modern day computer. He was convicted of being homosexual and had to choose between two years in prison or chemical castration. He chose the latter so that he could continue with his inventions. He finally committed suicide aged 41. How much more would he have invented and contributed for the benefit of society if he had lived in a more tolerant community? Although he eventually received a posthumous pardon from Queen Elizabeth many years later, in 2013, his genius was silenced in the most brutal manner.

I deliberately introduce the story of Alan Turing as his is not an isolated example and many gay people around the world have been subjected to various 'therapies' administered against their will.

Homosexuality remains a dischargeable offence in many armed forces around the world. It was only towards the end of the 20th century that attitudes towards homosexuality became more liberal. In South Africa male same-sex conduct was only legalized as recently as the 1990s. However, legalization did not mean acceptance by communities riddled with prejudice. During the apartheid years, homosexuality was a crime punishable by up to seven years in prison. The law was often used to harass and outlaw the gay community and gay events in South Africa.

Ours was not a liberal family and sex was never openly discussed, let alone homosexuality. The latter was perceived as unnatural and shameful, to say the least. We were also brought up with a deep respect for authority and the law in particular and Duimpie was petrified of doing anything that might be perceived as 'wrong' in the eyes of the law. He also had strong spiritual and religious leanings, and as religion played a key part in the majority of traditional communities in South Africa, they condemned homosexuality as a sin. His sense of guilt at being a gay man meant he continued to suppress his sexual orientation for many years.

Small town communities, especially those of white Afrikaners, were dominated by Calvinistic values that expected individuals to conform to the group norms. Difference was not encouraged, especially if it challenged the values and traditions of the community. For example, it was inconceivable that someone from the community would not be totally devoted to rugby, which is supported with an almost religious fervor. Imagine a rather feminine young boy not fighting to get into the school rugby team, but instead preferring to take music lessons. Prejudices extended beyond those of racial discrimination, and anyone who did not share the values of the dominant group was an outsider and was treated as such. Alas, prejudice is not found exclusively in one town, region or country, it is a worldwide phenomenon.

Our culture subscribed to the belief that authority was not challenged in any shape or form and children were to be seen and not heard. Children had to address anyone older than them by 10 years or so as Mr or Mrs, or 'auntie' or 'uncle' when known by the family. Daughters had to be obedient, become innocent brides, subservient wives, nurturing mothers and exemplary homemakers, supporting charitable activities often associated with the Dutch Reformed Church. No wife would dream of offering bought cakes, biscuits or any other bought refreshments to her guests, and the quality and quantity of her baking and cooking abilities defined her identity as a woman. Except when it came to barbecues or the traditional *braaivleis*. This was a man's task and the irony was lost on white, macho, beer-drinking men that, like women folk, they would proudly boast and compare the secrets of their barbecue sauce recipes around the fire. It would be the only time you would find a white Afrikaner male engaged in the preparation of food.

Such conservative social attitudes often led to aggression towards gay people, resulting in beatings by men from such groups who perceived it as their duty to rid society of homosexuals. Lesbians were both beaten and raped due to the perceived threat they posed to traditional male authority. Being of an artistic temperament, Duimpie had both a fear and abhorrence of aggression of any kind, which he saw as coarseness and a lack of refinement. It would not be unusual for an Afrikaner male from a more rural environment who dared to come out of the closet to be totally ostracized from both his family and his community. Duimpie's height and build offered some protection against such aggressive behavior, particularly in school. We both grew to our adult height in our early teens, which meant Duimpie was one of the tallest in his school.

Given the prejudices of these conservative communities, it was ironic, therefore, that South Africa was the first nation in the world to explicitly prohibit discrimination based on sexual orientation in its constitution. Even more ironic is the fact that the South African Police Force, which was composed of predominantly white Afrikaner men and which regularly raided gay events or clubs, now had to protect the rights of gay people in South Africa. In November 2006 the South African Parliament voted for a bill allowing same-sex civil marriage, which came just in time for Duimpie and Pieter. Intolerance towards gay people continues to persist to some degree in South Africa, especially outside the cities. However, in major urban areas they are now fairly well accepted and large cities have a thriving gay nightlife.

This was certainly not the case during Duimpie's youth. Being a gay man meant he always had to wear a mask when stepping into the world outside. It required a constant censorship of his identity, behavior and interactions with others. This is probably the main driver why Duimpie's home, no matter how small, was seen as his haven. He spent much of his time creating an aesthetically pleasing and creative environment and a sense of harmony that was so important to him. His home was the only place he could truly be himself and put away the masks reserved for the outside world. He could wear what he wanted and express himself by throwing his wrists around as much as he liked, with hands on hips and a dramatic flick of the head accompanied by a raised theatrical voice, without the fear of reprisal, ridicule or humiliation. As with so many gay people like him, he desperately tried to rid himself of his sexual orientation and conform to what was perceived as 'normal', whatever that means.

CHAPTER FOUR

Duimpie's friendship with Karen continued to flourish and therefore it came as no surprise when they eventually announced their intention to get married. I was as dismayed by the news as our father was ecstatic. It confirmed what he had always maintained, that with determination and the love of a good woman, my brother could overcome his unnatural tendencies. I did not doubt his good intentions, but I knew Duimpie was making the gravest mistake of his life.

As she was their only daughter, Karen's parents spared no expense and arranged a huge white wedding with all the trimmings and celebrations to go with it. The day went well and the bride and groom went off on their honeymoon amidst the cheers and good wishes of family and friends and the ubiquitous trailing of beer cans tied to the bridal car. I found this rather amusing, as Duimpie had never drunk beer in his life! However, much to my surprise he developed a taste for Murphy's ale when visiting the UK for the first time years later. He often referred to himself as a *moffie*, Afrikaans slang for being gay, so I would tease him and say he was a *Murphy moffie*. Sadly, I perceived the trailing beer cans as symbolic of the alien nature of the lifestyle on which he was embarking. The cheerful send-off did nothing to curb my foreboding and I waited with trepidation for them to return from honeymoon.

Upon their return, they moved into a house they were renting from the mining company that owned the hospital where Duimpie worked. On the surface life for them seemed to settle into what might be described as the life of a normal heterosexual married couple. They went to work, had my parents over for Sunday dinners, tended their garden, made friends and engaged in some of the social activities one would expect of a married couple. I have a vivid memory of visiting them one Saturday afternoon. As I drew up outside their house Duimpie was in the garden digging up borders, ready for planting some seasonal flowers. Nothing unusual about that, you would think, but the pain etched on his face and the fervor of his digging told another story. He was living a lie and he was desperately trying to be the married man and do what was expected of a married man.

Duimpie had been open and honest with Karen from the outset and she knew he was gay. She was clearly devoted to him and, like our father, firmly believed that she would be able to help rid him of his sexual orientation. However, I don't think she ever had a true grasp of what it meant for Duimpie to be gay, nor the emotional acrobatics he had to engage in to try to conform to and live the life of a heterosexual male. I sensed his deep unhappiness and helplessly stood by as a witness to the emotional torture he was putting himself through.

As was to be expected, it all came to a head about seven months after their wedding, when Duimpie broke down and admitted to Karen that he could no longer live the lie they had created. The inevitable outcome was speeded up by her insistence on trying to have a family. They were constantly being subjected to the veiled comments from friends and family who expected married life to eventually lead to the patter of small feet around the house. It would have been socially unacceptable not to have children. You got married and had children, end of story. Duimpie was horrified at the thought and he realized he could no longer continue with the charade. He cared deeply for Karen as a friend, but could not offer her the love and life she quite naturally wanted.

Understandably, she was devastated and even now, looking back, Duimpie unfairly took all the blame on himself, which Karen was happy for him to do. Gone was the loving, supportive and understanding wife, and there entered a woman scorned. The undoing of their marriage was as messy as a divorce can be. Guilt ridden and remorseful, my dearest brother gave everything to Karen and did nothing to defend himself against the accusations from all quarters, namely her family, friends and our father. Furthermore, Duimpie had to endure physical threats against him from her brother, and her family behaved in the typical manner expected of a traditionally conservative Afrikaner family at that time; one in which cultural values viewed aggression and physical violence, fueled by excessive male testosterone, as the only way to resolve differences.

Had Karen given Duimpie the opportunity to break the news to our parents in person, he might have been able to rescue his fragile relationship with our father. Instead, Karen decided to seek refuge with my parents after Duimpie told her that he was unable to continue with the masquerade. Given our father's values, he was never able to resist a damsel in distress and she played the role extremely well. For him it was black and white with no shades of grey as to where the blame lay. Was that an act of revenge from a woman scorned? Who knows, and if that was the case, she achieved her outcome admirably. Our father banished Duimpie from the family home and made sure he got the sack from his job. He was cast asunder without thought or consideration as to his own emotional state and wellbeing.

We were not allowed even to mention Duimpie's name in the house and under no circumstances were any of us allowed to make contact with him. However, I was never good at doing what I was told and had no intention of turning my back on my beloved brother. He took what remained of his personal belongings and his shattered emotions and confidence and returned to Pretoria, securing a post in the open-heart unit of the hospital where he had trained years earlier. The same matron still ruled the roost and, with a soft spot for Duimpie, she enabled him to be reinstated.

Duimpie worked as a psychiatric nurse for some years. He then trained as a theater sister and spent a number of years working with the teams performing open-heart surgery in Pretoria. Due to his dyslexia, structure and routine were very important to him, and since these were characteristics highly valued in theater, the environment suited him well.

Not only was he good at his job, but he was also a hard worker. His work ethic, together with his outgoing personality, meant he was always popular with the hospital management and his medical colleagues. His patients adored him and as far as Duimpie was concerned nothing was ever too much trouble for them and their families. Until the end of his career he lovingly cared for both his patients and their families, often going far beyond the call of duty. One of his colleagues gave him the nickname *Boetietjie* (pronounced boutiekie), which roughly translates as little brother. It was an endearment that stayed with him until the end, and patients and colleagues always referred to him as such. It was a sign of the affection and esteem in which he was held, including the fierce matron whose formidable demeanor would slip when she called Duimpie by this name.

He was incredibly tidy and organized, which were also skills that were highly valued in a hospital theater. Even when we were children, his cupboards and bedroom in general were constantly used as an example to me of what my room should look like, especially as I was a girl. When told to tidy up my room, I would merely throw everything lying on the floor into the cupboard and quickly shut the door, before it all came tumbling out again. Duimpie, on the other hand, spent ages making labels for his shelves with the contents immaculately stacked. This was not my idea of fun or a way of spending my spare time. As I was the tomboy, he would often insist on giving me a thorough scrub to get rid of the stains and dirt accumulated from a day spent outdoors. He would regularly lecture our mother on what she had to do in order to teach me how to behave like a lady. To me at that time, being a lady meant spending ages in the bathroom, a thought that filled me with horror.

After his exile, I continued to secretly communicate with Duimpie and occasionally had the opportunity to visit him. After some two years, our mother eventually persuaded our father to go and see Duimpie and make peace with him. There is no doubt, given our father's personality and values, that he would not have approached the encounter in any way other than intending to lay down the law; his law. It would have been accompanied by a number of conditions, including for Duimpie to change his ways if he was to be allowed back into the family fold. Having lived with the extreme consequences of attempting to conform to the role of a heterosexual male, Duimpie had finally come to accept that he was never going to be anything other than homosexual.

For the first time in his life Duimpie matched our father like for like with a no holds barred approach. He made it brutally clear that he had no intention of making any further compromises or attempts at conforming to our father's idea of a 'normal' son. I think secretly our father admired the fact that Duimpie stood up to him, and instead he was the one to be given an ultimatum: 'Accept me for what I am or forget that I am your son.' Our father capitulated and a truce was reached, much to the relief of the rest of the family. Slowly, over a long time, the family relationships were rebuilt and eventually our father came to accept Duimpie, although he would never condone his sexuality. In time, he became the one child in the family who was truly there with unconditional love and support when our parents needed it most. Like Duimpie, our father eventually succumbed to prostate cancer, except at a much later age than Duimpie was when he was diagnosed.

Nevertheless, acceptance of his sexuality meant that Duimpie was never overtly effeminate in public, except in the company of a few close friends when he would flap his wrists when excited and refer to everyone as 'doll'. He would always be conscious of how he came across in public and his behavior never revealed his homosexuality. Having said that, one didn't have to be a highly trained sleuth to detect his effeminate mannerisms, no matter how hard he tried to hide them. It was impossible to wholly suppress this side of him, but he expressed it in a way that did not offend or challenge others, especially heterosexual males. What a burden it was for a gay man at that time to be ever vigilant of not revealing the essence of his personality and always playing the role of someone else. How very exhausting!

For the first time in his life, Duimpie was more relaxed about being a gay man and, having come to accept himself, he was more comfortable about becoming involved in the gay scene, albeit on the fringes. He even introduced my family to some of his gay friends and as time went by our father came to enjoy the company of a number of his gay friends. Although it took much longer before he would openly admit to this! However, Duimpie's foray into the gay scene continued to be conservative and low key. It required my wicked influence later on to persuade him to be more adventurous and participate in gay social life, but more of this in later chapters.

CHAPTER FIVE

I first went to live with Duimpie after he had met the first male partner with whom he would publicly and openly share an apartment. This was some three years or so after the breakup with Karen. Dietmar was from a German family whose parents immigrated to South Africa when he was fairly young, and this background chimed with Duimpie's attraction to the German way of life. His father, a warm and caring man, was a Lutheran Minister from the German tradition. Dietmar was gorgeous! He was of average build, a bit shorter than Duimpie, with black hair touching his collar and a beautifully groomed black beard with expressive hazel eyes that would come alive and sparkle with intelligence and mischief when he was on a high.

As a bipolar sufferer, he could also have his very dark moments, which at such times made him almost unbearable to be with. When I first met him I thought what a waste that such a gorgeous hunk of a man was gay. The only consolation was that he was with my beloved brother and that Duimpie was clearly very happy and, for the first time, contented with being a gay man in a gay relationship. Although he wouldn't have dreamt of openly admitting it, our father was both surprised by and taken with Dietmar. Like so many other heterosexuals, our father firmly believed that all gay people frequented sleazy nightclubs every night and solicited boys in toilets. 'Pedophiles the lot of them!' he would mumble under his breath. Dietmar and Duimpie severely challenged his beliefs about gay couples; they actually lived ordinary lives just like the rest of society.

I got on really well with Dietmar and, after a year or so of them being together, they decided to move from Pretoria to Johannesburg and invited me to go and live with them and to share a large three bedroomed apartment in the Hillbrow area of the city. By this time, you will be able to guess the response of our father, but as I had anticipated this, I gave him no option to react in his usual manner. I was living with my parents at that time, which I found incredibly stifling and restrictive, and was desperate to escape the constraints of a rural, small town society. Our father controlled my comings and goings and on the rare occasions when I brought a boyfriend home, he would put the fear of God in him. Needless to say, my boyfriends were never good enough. They did not wear a tie, had a beard, did not know how to conduct themselves, had the wrong job, and so the list went on and on.

Duimpie and Dietmar visited us occasionally and, to give our father his due, he was polite towards Dietmar. I think the fact that he came from what our father termed 'a decent and educated family' gave him a reason for finding Dietmar acceptable and explained his mellower attitude towards them as a couple. He also knew that, should he make it difficult for Duimpie, he would not see him again and, for the sake of our mother, he was civil during their visits. However, he was not in favor of me visiting them too often or on my own, as he was convinced they would influence me to behave in inappropriate ways; whatever that meant.

So, on that particular morning I got up, drove off to work as normal, or so my parents thought. Instead I drove to Johannesburg and, having earlier made contact with the Human Resources Department of IBM on the off chance of a suitable vacancy, I was invited for an interview. Before I got home that afternoon, they had phoned and asked my mother to tell me I had got the job and to contact them with my acceptance and to arrange a start date. Of course, our mother knew nothing about a job interview! Before our father could recover from the shock, I had packed and was gone. For our father the shock was twofold. Firstly, I was going to live with my brother and his lover, and who knows to what I would be exposed. Secondly, he did not approve of Johannesburg and saw it as Sodom and Gomorrah where I could only be led astray if Duimpie and Dietmar didn't succeed in doing so first.

The three of us got on very well initially and we spent quite a bit of time renovating and decorating the apartment the way we wanted it. It was large with a beautiful view of Hillbrow. Our apartment block was built on a hill and was next to the then famous Ponte Towers, which was considered *the* place to live for the privileged, mainly white classes of

Johannesburg. I loved it! Hillbrow was on what was seen as the edge of the city at that time, although the city has morphed over the years. It was a vibrant and metropolitan community with continental style cafés, an all night supermarket that sold items I had not even heard of before, a theater and wonderful restaurants. It was a buzzing community of artists and intellectuals and was also one of the first identifiable gay and lesbian areas in urban South Africa. I felt safe and quite comfortable going out on my own at night. I felt so grown-up and also loved my job with IBM, which was a terrific company to work for. Duimpie and I both thrived; we had found our natural habitat. It was like stumbling on an oasis having wandered around the desert for a long time, strangled by the bigoted and narrow-minded beliefs of the small town communities in which we were brought up.

One of the important things that brought Duimpie and Dietmar together was a shared value of spirituality. Dietmar, with his religious background, was a member of the American branch of the Lutheran Church. Its members had a much more inclusive and liberal attitude towards individuals or groups who were perceived as different to their more traditional brethren from the Dutch Reformed Church in whose traditions we were raised. Not only did this include a more liberal view of gay people, but also a more questioning and discursive approach to religion. We were active members of the Church and we spent much of our time involved in the various activities organized by the local church, including contributing to the various church committees. We even took part in running Sunday School classes, which was a very rewarding and enjoyable experience.

Duimpie blossomed and as always became a well-loved member of the church community and would often share his musical talents by playing the organ during services or at different social events and musical evenings organized by the various committees. It was a very happy time and we were part of a broadminded and inclusive group that neither Duimpie nor I had been exposed to until then. The majority of the congregation were English-speaking South Africans from the city and therefore had an intellectual attitude and a less prejudiced outlook than the more rural, Afrikaner communities.

Our upbringing was somewhat different from others in our communities. Our mother's family came from Switzerland and she always had different ideas from those of others in our immediate environment. Our father was also brought up in an English-speaking culture in what was the Cape Province at the time of his birth. When he was around nine years old he moved with his mother to the region near Johannesburg now known as Gauteng. We therefore did not follow the traditional behaviors or reflect the values of others in the immediate communities we lived in, especially in the more rural parts of the country. We also spoke a mixture of English, Dutch and sometimes German.

A key example of such a difference was how our mother would actively encourage us, including me as the girl in the family, to go out and explore the world and engage with new experiences and different people. This was such an anathema to others in the community, especially for girls. I spent many years as a child going for orthodontic treatment in Johannesburg, often by train and naturally accompanied by our mother. When I was 10 years old, she decided I was old enough to look after myself and encouraged me to travel by myself. Her sense of adventure and love of life no doubt helped to fuel my desire to explore and embrace the wider world with all the opportunities of different experiences and cultures it had to offer. To say friends and others in the community were horrified that I was allowed to travel to the big city on my own at such a young age was an understatement! How our mother ever persuaded our father that it was an acceptable idea, I still do not know to this day.

Sadly, in later years, after the end of apartheid, all that Johannesburg and Hillbrow had to offer changed. It became a place where one did not dare enter with or without armed bodyguards. It was reported that even the police kept their distance. Poor infrastructural planning meant Hillbrow in particular couldn't cope with a rapidly expanding population. The significant influx of immigrants from other parts of Africa resulted in a significant increase in xenophobic crime against such foreigners.

During the apartheid years, from 1948 to 1994, one of the main reasons for military conscription was the Border War, or commonly known as the Angolan Bush War. The conflict was focused mainly in South West Africa, now Namibia, and on the border with Angola. The conflict was between South Africa and Angola, supported by its allied forces, and was closely connected to the civil war ravaging Angola during that time, as well as the Namibian war of independence. The patrol of the South African borders was also to prevent illegal entry by migrants and other foreigners. The scale and presence of border control by the South African Defence Force was scaled down post-apartheid. However, a redeployment of a military presence on the borders is now under way in response to the wave of migration into South Africa as well as protecting the borders against any international threats.

The continued influx of immigrants seeking refuge or jobs in South Africa has led to a significant rise in squatter camps, particularly near cities and towns. This has resulted in overcrowding, poverty, poor service delivery, lack of housing and, as is to be expected, a lack of employment. The consequences are a disparity between rich and poor that can only lead to crime and violence. The efforts of the Truth and Reconciliation Commission offered hope in the reduction of violence, but alas it has failed to address its escalation post-1994.

In addition, there was a mass exodus of middle class residents to new urban areas in the 1980s, taking their investment resources with them, and eventually Hillbrow became an urban slum. Instead, the gangs moved in and the crime rate rocketed after the end of apartheid. Many of the apartment buildings were hijacked by gangs and taken from legitimate landlords. The crime statistics, especially the increase in drug-related crime, would suggest that despite a successful transition into a constitutional state, South Africa is not able to protect the rights, freedoms and privileges of many of its citizens nor those of the foreign migrants. This is made worse given that the perpetrators of the most violent crimes do not subscribe to any known civilized boundaries. During the 1990s you could guarantee that you would be mugged at the very least if you entered Hillbrow.

There has been some change but rubbish continues to rot in the alleys with sewage running down main streets from illegally occupied buildings.

Eventually, as with other residents, Duimpie and Dietmar decided to buy a house in suburbia near the hospital where they both worked. Dietmar, like Duimpie, was a qualified psychiatric sister, which is how they originally met. I moved with them but became increasingly disillusioned with Dietmar's treatment of Duimpie, especially during his down times. He would be one of the most interesting and fun loving people to be with when on a high, but his down periods were very dark and destructive, not only to himself but to others as well. Despite his knowledge he lacked personal insight into how severe his ups and downs could be during the times he stopped taking his medication. Duimpie, with his natural caring disposition and psychiatric training, was convinced he would be the right partner to support Dietmar, but it was not to be. Even Duimpie's love and understanding could not drive out the demons that plagued Dietmar. The source of some of these demons was the guilt he felt at being a gay man, especially coming from an old German family and with a German Lutheran Minister as a father.

Not long after we moved into the house, I left. I was also concerned that Duimpie might be staying because of me so I thought it best to give him the space to decide what was the right thing for him to do. Finally, Dietmar drove Duimpie away and he also left, once again, with only his personal possessions. On the day he left he made an oath that it would be the last time he would leave his home with nothing but a suitcase of personal belongings. As it turned out, this relationship paled into insignificance in comparison with the deep commitment and love he eventually found with Pieter. Duimpie moved into an apartment owned by the private hospital he was then working for and I joined him shortly after. We lived there together for a few years before I finally left South Africa.

Duimpie and I shared a common sense of not belonging in South Africa, particularly within the more rural conservative Afrikaner communities. To help understand why this was the case, I'll provide a brief background into how these communities came about and the factors that influenced the emergence of their particular culture. As I suggested earlier, these communities had clearly defined values that dictated behaviors within their community boundaries. Historically, South Africa became divided between two camps, namely the Dutch- and English-speaking groups. During the early 1900s a large group of Dutch-speaking inhabitants started the migration inland and away from the Cape Province dominated by the British. It was known as 'The Great Trek'.

There were many reasons for the exodus, a major one being the British and their language law of 1806. The overriding purpose of the law was an attempt by the British to convert the European settlers, a large majority of them Dutch, to the English language and its culture. Prior to the arrival of the British, education, justice and trade were conducted in Dutch. Of particular importance was the conducting of church services in Dutch. The Dutch settlers were very religious and any attempt at suppressing the use of their language and the use of the Dutch Reformed bible was a sensitive issue, fueling dissent. The influence of the Dutch Reformed Church in rural Afrikaner communities remains strong. All of these issues combined to create a divide and tension between the English- and Dutch-speaking settlers that is still evident in South African society today. The divide between the two groups is kept alive through a separate English and Afrikaner education system, including schools, colleges and universities.

The Afrikaners come from a strong line of pastoral stock, relying on religious leadership from the early days of their Dutch forefathers. In time the language, as well as its people, came to be associated with the apartheid policies, social exclusion and injustice. On the other hand English became the language of the opposition. Afrikaans, the language of the Afrikaner, is a symbol of their cultural identity, and from 1948 until independence Afrikaners more or less dominated politics in South Africa. Conversely, the English held more sway in commerce and education. As I've already indicated, Afrikaans is associated with the more rural population and the ideology of nationalism whereas the English language is associated with a more international and liberal urban community.

Under the South African Constitution of 1996 Afrikaans, together with English and nine other languages, remains an official language. Afrikaans continues to be a strong and vibrant language and probably one of the reasons why many Dutch and Belgian companies outsourced their call centers to South Africa. Afrikaans speakers are able to learn the Dutch language quickly with little training. As a point of interest, there has been a significant revival in Afrikaans-language cinema, with *Skoonheid* being the first Afrikaans film to be screened at the Cannes Film Festival, in 2011. As a matter of fact, the film industry touched the lives of Duimpie and Pieter in a significant way towards the end of Duimpie's life. I will say more of that later.

I have sketched a very simplistic picture of the English and Afrikaans communities and their people, and no culture is ever that one dimensional or easy to define. Any culture is a product of many layers of complexity woven into its rich heritage created over many generations. Furthermore, neither of these communities can be studied in isolation as to who and what they have become and how they continue to evolve. They can only be understood through their joint evolution with many of the black cultures and communities with whom they have lived side by side over the turbulent and sometimes violent history of Southern Africa.

However, it might give you some insight as to why neither Duimpie nor I were able to conform to what we perceived to be the restrictions and expectations of the rural Afrikaner society. We often found ourselves in such communities due to our father's profession. Some of the mines he was responsible for were located within rural Southern Africa. We experienced it as a culture designed by white men for white men, and everyone else (black, colored, female, gay, etc.) had to conform to the standards they literally imposed upon them.

This is why we felt so liberated during the times we lived in Hillbrow. It was a culture within a culture and one that was so much more attuned to our own personal values. I had always known that I would leave South Africa and I failed to persuade Duimpie to join me. Unlike me, he didn't have the courage to break away and he capitulated to our upbringing, advocating a steady job, with a pension at the end of it, and although there is nothing wrong with this belief, it wasn't for me. There was a world waiting to be explored and different cultures to be experienced.

CHAPTER SIX

However, before finally leaving South Africa, Duimpie and I once again enjoyed the thrill of being back in Hillbrow. It was like the old times and we had such fun together, picking up where we had left off. We had returned to the environment and society with its unique culture that we loved. As far as we were concerned, we had come home. We felt once again liberated to express ourselves without constraint or being ever watchful of overstepping rigid and limiting social boundaries. We thrived in the vibrant cosmopolitan environment that suited us so well. We would often go for a coffee in a café at night, especially after a movie, and just sit and talk for hours, watching life pulsate until the early hours of the morning before going home. It truly was an island within a big ocean.

As an alternative to going out, one of our favorite pastimes would be to boil condensed milk for about four hours until it turned to deliciously sweet caramel. We would burn our mouths as we couldn't wait for it to cool down before getting stuck in with teaspoons, and inevitably suffered from overindulgence afterwards. Duimpie had a knack, just before I fell asleep, of popping the question 'What would you do if you won a million Rand?' (South African currency). That was enough to ensure I was instantly wide awake and we would then spend the next hour or two dreaming about what we would do with the money. Looking back, such fortune would not have been possible as it was in the days before any form of lottery. However, it provided us with many hours of entertainment.

As it happens, Duimpie's dream of winning on the lottery did come true, although not such a significant win. While visiting me in England on one of his trips, he had bought a lottery ticket. It was with great excitement and anticipation that we watched the balls roll down the shoot. We couldn't believe it when one after the other his numbers appeared! Although the win was only £1700 and was not going to lead to a life of riches, the anticipation and excitement was enough for us. Our dream had come true; we had finally achieved the thrill of winning on the lottery.

Another of our favorite pastimes was to play rich. We loved going into 'town', as Johannesburg was referred to despite being a big city, and spent many hours enjoying the delights of beautifully displayed items in the various shop windows. We would press our faces close to the glass, pontificating for ages about where we would place the items in our small apartment, if we could afford to buy them. We both had a love of beautiful things, whether they were to be found in nature, art, or beauty expressed in any other form. Duimpie was particularly sensitive to being surrounded by beautiful objects, which he used to say 'created harmony and tranquility that feeds the soul'. It made him physically ill and depressed if his surroundings jarred aesthetically in any way, or lacked taste.

In our early days together, Duimpie was a student nurse and my career had just started. We did not have a great deal of spare cash between us and we would often scrape together our limited funds to go for coffee at the then illustrious Carlton Hotel and its famous Die Koffiehuis (The Coffee House). It was by far our most favorite place for coffee and on occasions a piece of cake when our meager reserves would stretch that far. We could never compromise quality for quantity and would rather enjoy one unforgettable trip a month to our special coffee shop as opposed to four at a lesser establishment. It was a coffee shop cum informal restaurant and part of the renowned five star Carlton Hotel situated in the center of Johannesburg. We loved the décor of the hotel, with its wood paneling, rich colors and luscious carpets, and the outstanding service for which it was well known. The hushed surroundings so appealed to our sense of beauty and luxury. If we felt particularly flush or managed to make savings elsewhere, we would indulge in one of the mouthwatering breakfast dishes that reflected the quality of dining elsewhere in the hotel.

After I joined IBM the Carlton Hotel became my preferred destination for breakfast and occasionally a drink after work. It was directly opposite the IBM building and became known as 'Little IBM' although the building was anything but little. I shall never forget my induction at IBM when on my first day my line manager announced that the company tradition was that a new employee was always taken for lunch as a welcome to the company. It was the task of my immediate supervisor to accompany me on the welcome lunch at one of the restaurants in the Carlton Hotel. I couldn't wait to get home to share my experience with Duimpie. Until then we had only dreamt of an opportunity to dine in the Carlton.

A welcome lunch was not the only thing I was introduced to, and having lived a very sheltered life, particularly when it came to alcohol, I encountered Kahlúa coffee for the first time and became a convert there and then. For anyone not familiar with the drink, it is made from the coffee liqueur called Kahlúa. Another first was a business lunch that went on until the late afternoon. Those were the days!

The Carlton Hotel, designed to resemble an upside down Y shape, was once a rich status symbol for South Africa and the hotel was internationally renowned for its fine dining and quality of service. The famous nightclub, The Top of the Carlton, located on the 50th floor, offered a breathtaking view of the sights of Johannesburg, especially at night with the twinkling lights of the city far below. The hotel played host to the world's most popular entertainers, politicians and celebrities and over its 25 year history it entertained visitors such as Henry Kissinger, François Mitterand, Margaret Thatcher, Whitney Houston, Mick Jagger and many others. The famous Three Ships restaurant was internationally known for its outstanding cuisine. During its existence, the hotel made a significant contribution to developing the international careers of many top hoteliers and chefs. Sadly, the once glittering iconic building closed its doors in 1997 as it became too dangerous for guests to stay there. As soon as guests ventured into the surrounding streets they would more than likely be mugged and in those days the center of Johannesburg became an area not even the most foolhardy ventured into.

An underground shopping center linked the hotel to the Carlton Centre, a skyscraper housing offices and shops that boasted of being the tallest office building in Africa for 41 years. After being empty for some years, the city center is slowly coming back to life with investment once again finding its way into the city. A number of factors contributed to the decline of the Carlton Centre, including the worldwide economic downturn. However, problems closer to home such as the rise in violent crime resulted in the exodus of business moguls from the center to safer surrounding areas. However, before its demise the Carlton was one of our favorite places to go and we dreamt of the day we could afford to dine in the glamorous Three Ships Restaurant.

I would often be the token female for Duimpie and some of our gay friends when they had to attend social functions that expected them to be accompanied by a woman. On one of these occasions Duimpie and I went to the Christmas party at the hospital where he worked. A few weeks prior to the party, I spotted a particularly beautiful cocktail dress, which at that time was far beyond my means. Every time we went past the boutique I would dream of owning the dress. It was made of beautiful cream chiffon with long puff sleeves, sunray pleats and pink hibiscus flowers printed on the hem. Underneath was a very simple cream satin sheath with shoelace straps.

My birthday was a couple of days before the Christmas party and on the day of my birthday Duimpie presented me with an exquisite oblong box, tied with pink silk ribbons. I was speechless and so excited to find out what the delicate box could possibly contain. Upon lifting the lid, there were layers of delicate tissue paper that I slowly unfolded with trembling fingers. When I finally lifted the last layer I gasped as the very dress I had coveted for weeks was revealed, neatly folded up in more layers of pink tissue paper. I was so overwhelmed by Duimpie's generosity as I knew he would have scrimped and saved for a long time to buy the dress. He would have gone without many necessities in order to afford it.

Such was the generosity of his nature and it was also representative of the close relationship we shared. We would do anything necessary if it meant giving the other one something they really wanted or that would bring them joy and pleasure. I felt like Cinderella going to the ball on the evening of the party. I wore that dress for many years until it literally fell apart and it broke my heart to eventually part with it. My sadness was not only in losing the pleasure of wearing the dress, but more importantly as a symbol of the memories it brought back of the special relationship Duimpie and I had shared and his boundless generosity.

On another occasion it was my opportunity to do something special for Duimpie and to say it turned out to be quite a memorable evening would be an understatement. I decided to spend the equivalent of my whole month's salary taking him out for dinner at the Three Ships Restaurant and I had to book months in advance to secure a table. I probably spent just as long saving up the money to pay for it. The occasion was to celebrate his 33rd birthday and it was also the last significant occasion we would spend together before I left South Africa.

We felt like royalty when, with grace, the maître d' showed us to our table. We could hardly believe that we were finally realizing the moment we had dreamt of for so long. Often we would come into the Carlton and just stop and stare at the dimly lit interior of the Three Ships, exuding luxury, promising ourselves that one day we would be sitting at one of the tables with its starched white tablecloth, array of silver cutlery and numerous crystal glasses. The experience was everything and more than we had expected.

Seated next to us were what appeared to be two businessmen deep in conversation. Halfway through our meal one of the men turned to us and enquired, in an accent I could not place, whether we were celebrating a special occasion. His manner and the way in which he asked the question indicated that he thought we were a couple. I replied yes and said we were there to celebrate my brother's birthday. He responded enthusiastically in a very different tone of voice and insisted that the maître d' arrange for a cake to be brought in honor of Duimpie's birthday. This he duly did and accompanied the presentation of the beautifully decorated chocolate cake with 'Happy Birthday' sung by the waiters.

The manner in which our new acquaintances were treated by the staff suggested they were regulars at the hotel. Our fellow diners insisted after dinner that we joined them in The Top of the Carlton for champagne as part of Duimpie's birthday celebrations. By this time my poor brother was getting very uncomfortable and muttered to me under his breath, 'How on earth are we going to pay for all that?' It was well known that the nightclub was reserved for the rich and famous, with deep pockets to match, a description that certainly did not apply to us. I tried to allay my brother's fears and told him to relax and enjoy the evening in his honor and that, 'After all, we were invited, which would suggest they'll pick up the tab for the nightclub.' Duimpie wasn't totally convinced but reluctantly went along, as he had always wanted to see the view from the top.

It is true to say that the view was breathtaking and lived up to its reputation. There were 360-degree views from floor to ceiling glass windows that overlooked the sparkling lights of the city. Dotted around the room were intimate alcoves discreetly hidden, offering privacy, as well as more public seating areas with tables positioned around the dance floor. The lights were subdued and deep purple carpets covered the floor away from the dancing area. We sank into soft sofas with a small table in the center of the seating area reserved for the drinks.

One of the businessmen ordered a bottle of Dom Pérignon champagne, and even with my limited knowledge of champagne, I knew it came with a price tag way outside of our budget. I was beginning to share Duimpie's apprehension, but I was not going to spoil the evening for him and was doing some quick thinking as to how I was going to cover some of the costs. I wondered whether the hotel would allow me to pay it off in installments; highly unlikely, my logical and sensible mind was trying to tell my more impulsive and mischievous inner child.

The champagne arrived in a freestanding ice bucket and the waiter went through all of the requisite ritual that should accompany the serving of a champagne of this quality. I had just taken a sip when one of our companions insisted that we join the other couples on the dance floor. I happily agreed as I have always enjoyed dancing. It was when we returned to our table that I lost my footing and, as I instinctively reached out for support, I sent the ice bucket together with its expensive contents flying across the carpeted floor. My poor brother nearly had palpitations. Our hosts thought nothing of it and promptly ordered a second bottle while discreet staff, appearing from nowhere, quickly whisked away the debris.

At this stage Duimpie was clutching the uncut chocolate birthday cake the restaurant had presented him with earlier at the dining table as though his life depended on it. In due course the bill arrived for our meals, the cost of entering the nightclub as well as the two bottles of champagne, which made both my brother and I gasp in horror. We had never been confronted with a bill of this size, which easily exceeded both our annual salaries. Before we could recover our composure and attempt to find a way of scraping together our contribution for the meal, one of our benefactors presented his room key and told the waiter to put the bill on his account. He waved away our feeble protests, insisting it was their way of saying thank you for our company and for livening up what would otherwise have been another evening discussing business. I never did quite get to the bottom of what business they were in or where they were from, but they were certainly lavish with their business expenses, much to our relief.

When we finally extricated ourselves from our wealthy benefactors, we made our way home and sat in the middle of Duimpie's bed eating chocolate cake at three in the morning. Our laughter had a hint of hysteria about it when reliving the events of the evening. Duimpie, always afraid of doing the wrong thing and getting into trouble, excitedly shared his fears, convinced that we were going to get into trouble over the champagne I had upset and the mounting cost of the evening's entertainment. He had visions of us spending the rest of our natural lives washing the dishes to try and recover the costs or, worse still, ending up in jail and having to contact our father to come and bail us out. We couldn't decide which of the two options would have been worse. It was certainly a memorable evening and we would often relive those memories in years to come.

Another love we shared was that of beautiful clothes and I enjoyed nothing more than going into boutiques and trying on gorgeous outfits. Our father had a strong dress sense and our mother taught fashion design and dressmaking. I suppose it was therefore inevitable that we inherited a love of clothes. I eventually found a boutique from where I bought most of my clothes, an experience Duimpie and I always looked forward to. One of the reasons for my choice of boutique was that they imported most of their range from Europe. Some of my fondest memories of our times together were of our trips there. It was much more than merely shopping for clothes, it was an experience, and we would very often return without having bought anything.

We made an occasion of these trips when we went on a Saturday morning to try on some of the items they had set aside for me. We became very good friends with Roz, one of the sales assistants, who would contact me when they received items she thought would be of interest to me. Roz would settle Duimpie in a chair, armed with a pot of coffee, and I would then try out the various outfits. We would discuss at length which, if any, would be suitable and, more importantly, affordable. By this time I had a well-established and fairly reasonably paid career with IBM. Up until then we'd had to make do with playing rich.

Another one of my favorite shops in which I indulged in such fantasies was a boutique selling leather and fur coats. As an animal lover, I would never have worn a fur coat, but I would have stretched to leather or sheepskin. On one of our sojourns to a very upmarket boutique, strolling in nonchalantly, I was particularly drawn to a reversible coat made from ostrich leather and black karakul pelt. The karakul is a breed of sheep reared in Namibia and known for its unique, tightly curled pelt. The sheep were brought to Namibia by the early German settlers during the 20th century.

I was always attracted to ostrich leather due to its unusual pattern of bumps or vacant quill follicles and I asked to try on this particular coat. My brother failed miserably to keep a straight face when it dawned on the shop assistant that she might have a sale. He bravely tried to hide his hysteria behind a coughing fit. The coat would have been equal to approximately $30,000 or more at today's value, and she could not have been more attentive. In order to extricate ourselves from the eager sales assistant, I haughtily declared that I didn't think it was my color and we summarily made our exit. It was one of those occasions when we were rendered helpless for a good 20 minutes afterwards by the fits of laughter that consumed us as soon as we left the shop.

In this chapter I have shared just some of the precious memories I had the privilege of experiencing with Duimpie over our earlier years together. We would have the opportunity to share many more wonderful memories in Europe after I left South Africa in the early 1980s. However, these were special times as we were still young with big dreams about what life held in store for us. Alas, our dreams took us in different directions and many of Duimpie's dreams were never realized due to the cancer that ended his life far too early. However, the bond that we shared never weakened after our separation and we continued to trade thoughts and experiences over the years. With the introduction of technology this was so much easier and, as both Pieter and I were early adopters of the new technology, we were able to email each other regularly with updates on our daily lives and chats on Skype when the then emerging Internet allowed.

Duimpie and I both had a strong sense of being born in the wrong place and an overwhelming feeling of being outsiders and mere visitors in South Africa. We shared a burning desire to move to Europe. This would be fuelled by visits from our mother's family from Switzerland and stories from the various expats living in South Africa. We would spend hours scheming and dreaming of starting a life together somewhere in Europe. Thanks to my mother's Swiss parentage we were able to speak German and, like most South Africans, we were also fluent in English and Afrikaans. This meant there were a number of countries to which we could easily have emigrated. Alas, it was a dream Duimpie never realized, but one I pursued two years or so after we returned to Hillbrow.

CHAPTER SEVEN

Being gay in South Africa in the late 1970s and early '80s still meant living a relatively covert existence, particularly within the more conservative Afrikaner communities. It was not uncommon for gay men and women to be targeted by brutish macho men who thought they could beat their sexual orientation out of them. It was because of this threat, and the fear of being rounded up in a police raid in a gay nightclub or bar, that Duimpie never frequented such places. One of Duimpie's friends, Barry, shared a funny story Duimpie once told him about one of his earlier attempts at socializing in gay nightclubs in his student days in Pretoria.

Under the apartheid government gay men were referred to as 'sodomites' and as it was illegal to be gay, just being in a gay nightclub might have led to being arrested. Even as late as the 1990s, there were frequent police raids with *moffies* scattering in all directions away from 'Betty Bangles' (as the police were called in gay parlance). So Duimpie, scraping up the courage and psyching himself up for the great event, went with some friends to a dark and shady, hidden gay club, as they all were in those days. It was his very first introduction to gay nightlife, and as luck would have it, lo and behold, not long after their arrival, in walked a couple of Betty Bangles.

We had been brought up with an almost reverent respect for any form of authority. So at the sight of the police, Duimpie went into panic mode and survival instinct kicked in. A thousand scenarios flashed before his eyes; from being beaten by the police, thrown into jail, sacked from the hospital and thrown off his nursing course, not to mention having to face the wrath of our father. With adrenaline pumping he made a dash for the bathroom and miraculously managed to squeeze his tall frame through the window of the toilet cubicle. A well-known mental institute was not far away and he ran as fast as his legs would carry him to the hospital. He made his way into the gardens, pacing up and down for a very long time in the hope that, if spotted by the police, they would consider him one of the residents. After what appeared to be an eternity pretending to be one of the patients, he returned home only to find that the police were merely there looking for one particular person, that it was not a raid and everyone else in the club had been left in peace. However, the experience left a psychological scar, which meant Duimpie didn't go near another gay club for a very long time.

You would be absolutely right if by now you have come to the conclusion that Duimpie was conservative in his public behavior. In fact, he was a self-confessed prude and I schemed and planned to get him out and about, meeting fellow gay men in the hope that he would meet someone to replace Dietmar. These were the days before Internet dating. In any case Duimpie would not have entertained doing such a thing under any circumstances. We would often have stand up arguments in clothes shops as he didn't want to buy anything he considered too gregarious or loud, thereby attracting unwanted attention. I vividly remember one such occasion when we had a good five-minute heated debate while I tried to persuade him to buy a beautiful double breasted tweed jacket in lovely autumn hues which perfectly complemented his coloring. I distinctly remember the shop assistant's head bobbing from one side to the other like someone at a tennis match, eagerly waiting to see who would win the point. I'm pleased to say I won, game, set and match, and that jacket became one of his most cherished pieces of clothing.

I was determined to continue with his education and modernization by getting him out and about, mixing with fellow gay men. The only way I was going to achieve this was by accompanying him to the more upmarket and well-known gay nightclubs in Johannesburg. There was one particular club considered to be the flagship of gay nightlife, called the Dungeon. Early on in its existence it introduced a drag queen contest, entitled 'Miss Dungeon', which it has held every year since then, I believe. It would feature drag acts from the most outrageous to the most gorgeous I have ever seen. They put the famous Dame Edna Everage to shame, the character created by the Australian comedian Barry Humphries, which became a popular and well-loved British drag act. The club was open to men and women and was particularly popular with lesbians, which made it easy for me to accompany Duimpie as I was able to blend in with the other partygoers.

However, not all clubs were inclusive to both sexes and I vividly recall on one occasion the lengths we went to in order to gain entry to an exclusive men only gay bar. I tried to go as a man in drag in the hope that it would hide the fact that I was actually a woman; a double bluff one might say. My drag outfit came complete with a smoking pipe. I was both a cigar and pipe smoker at the time, a feminine looking pipe, I hasten to add. The style was referred to as a Churchwarden pipe. It had a small bowl and a long, elegantly shaped stem. I was very pleased with my disguise when I initially managed to fool the doorman. However, despite being tall, it wasn't long before I was spotted as an imposter and summarily evicted from the premises. My poor Duimpie, another heart stopping experience for him and the conviction that we would end up in jail before the night was out. Fun we most certainly had *and* we managed to stay out of jail.

I am delighted to say that, despite my numerous interventions, Duimpie managed to meet the man of his dreams without my bumbling matchmaking efforts. When he met Pieter, it was love at first sight for both of them. They often shared with me how they felt when they first met. Both had an overwhelming sense that this was the real thing. By now Duimpie had moved to the town where our parents would finally settle and at last he had managed to buy his first home, which he christened *Nessie*, translated as little nest. The name indicated just how much having a safe haven, or nest, meant to him.

There was a sense of déjà vu for both Duimpie and our parents as it was the town where we lived at the time when our eldest brother died in the plane crash.

On the particular day Duimpie and Pieter met, Duimpie was tearing around his ward at breakneck speed with a greater sense of urgency than normal. However, given his long legs a brisk walking stride for him would be a running pace for anyone else. He was in a particular hurry to complete his ward rounds and was making sure everything was in perfect order before handing over to his colleagues on the next shift. Duimpie was always very conscientious and wanted to ensure there was nothing outstanding from his shift for his colleagues to deal with when they followed him on duty.

Despite his demanding nursing career, he had offered to provide nursing support to a friend, William, who had had an operation and was recovering at home. Duimpie mainly spent a few evenings with William as his friend could afford private nursing care during the day. So, that day he was in a rush to fulfil his nursing duties to William. Having finished work he left the hospital and made his way to *Boontjies*, or Little Bean as he had nicknamed his bright orange VW Beetle. On his way to William's house, he stopped to pick up some supplies for his friend and a box of his favorite chocolates. As he let himself in through the front door and made his way to William's bedroom, he was greeted by a strained 'hello' from William, pain visible on his face. Brightly, Duimpie suggested, 'You look so much better today, doll, with even a glow in your cheeks!'

Duimpie was fond of calling everyone 'doll', or 'bitch' if one of his gay friends was particularly sharp tongued. He suggested that he could hold his own with the best of them 'having gone to the finishing school for bitches, you know!', he would say, accompanied by a sweeping hand gesture for dramatic effect. As he said, 'There is nothing as bitchy as a bunch of flapping queens together.' Our father never lost his suspicions that mixing with Duimpie and his gay friends would have a detrimental impact on me. Who knows, their influence might even lead me astray to embrace a gay lifestyle. Despite his disapproval, however, I spent a lot of time with Duimpie and his friends. I so loved the sharp wit and barbed comments they would often hurl at each other. It was as though I had my own, personal cabaret show and spent many hours just sitting and listening to their banter and accompanied flapping of the wrists and dramatic gestures. I digress.

'I don't feel particularly rosy,' William groaned as he struggled to prop himself up against the numerous pillows that supported him in an upright sitting position in bed. 'You will feel much better after the delicious supper I'll be preparing for us in a minute,' Duimpie suggested, 'followed by a box of your favorite chocolates.' His comment prompted William to inform Duimpie that an old friend had called and would be joining them for dinner, if that was OK with him. Needless to say, it was, as Duimpie always enjoyed meeting new people. Little did he know that he was about to meet the man of his dreams and would never give another man a second glance for the remainder of his life.

When the front door bell rang, William asked

Duimpie to invite Pieter in, as it was no doubt going to be the friend he had invited for dinner. Duimpie opened the door and was speechless, something my brother rarely suffered from. Pieter recalled later that, 'The moment the door opened there was a bright white light which enveloped Duimpie, leaving me speechless and wholly in love.' This was a sensation shared by Duimpie and, for him, time stood still and he couldn't tear his eyes away from Pieter. He knew he had found the man of his dreams and his legs turned to jelly, threatening to give way under him. Eventually it was William calling out, 'Is that Pieter? Why has it gone so quiet?' that brought them back to reality. It was an immediate connection and a bond was forged during those brief moments that would only be severed by death. From that day onwards they were rarely apart and so a 23-year partnership began.

CHAPTER EIGHT

In many ways Pieter was very different from Duimpie; opposites do attract, as the saying goes. Pieter is quiet and introverted, preferring not to be the focus of attention and happy to give that privilege to someone other than himself. He was therefore always content for Duimpie to take center stage and to play the supporting role, which he did with so much love, commitment and dedication. Once you get to know Pieter you discover a very warm and loyal personality with a delightfully wicked sense of humor. Unlike Duimpie, who could be emotional and easily excited, Pieter remained calm in a crisis and preferred to use logic rather than emotion to deal with life's challenges. His calm and even disposition would become the lifesaving harbor from the stormy seas for Duimpie in times to come.

Pieter is a natural academic and has dedicated most of his working career to teaching children with special needs or from socially deprived backgrounds. Long before the end of the apartheid regime, Pieter forfeited a career in a mainstream white only school and dedicated his talents to working in a black only school in one of the townships where blacks had to live during the apartheid era. Black townships were normally built on the edge of towns and cities and were urban living areas reserved for blacks only. Segregation dates back to the colonial days when the British colonial government resettled racial groups. In the decades to follow subsequent governments restricted the rights of the non-white population in many ways, including where they lived. Townships became the mechanism for housing the non-white population with separate dwelling places being established across the country.

Alas, townships remain as perilous now as they were during the apartheid rule. Access to healthcare, education and transport remains inadequate to say the least. The purpose of the Reconstruction and Development Program, a government incentive established post-apartheid, was to build houses to accommodate the growing population in and around squatter camps. However, they are possibly worse than the original dwellings built during the apartheid era. They are built in the middle of nowhere without supporting infrastructure. Shoddy workmanship and inferior building materials have resulted in crumbling and cracked housing, which has become known as dog kennels, or worse.

Whoever Pieter interacts with, whether children in the classroom, friends, family or Duimpie, he offers total loyalty and commitment to those he cares for. This is evident in the way he lived with, and supported, his mother when he lost his father at a young age. Until his mother passed away, Pieter and

Duimpie split their time between the house Pieter shared with his mother and the house Duimpie bought with the support of our father. Although the arrangement had its own challenges, they made it work, and as Duimpie's house was often a building site, having Pieter's house to escape to offered a perfect solution.

Over the years Pieter's loyalty has extended beyond Duimpie and well and truly encompassed our small family. My father was diagnosed with prostate cancer in his seventies, and when Duimpie was at work and unable to rearrange his working hours, Pieter would be the one to take our father for his chemotherapy and hospital appointments. Over time his quiet demeanor earned him the respect and affection of our father. Towards the end of our mother's life she developed dementia and it was again Pieter who supported my sister to make the necessary arrangements for her care in an appropriate care home. Despite his own busy schedule, he would visit our mother every other day and continued to support my sister with all the official paperwork that needed attention. When our mother passed away it was Pieter who helped to make all the arrangements, including the complexities of dealing with her estate. He continues to be there for my sister as a source of support when needed.

At last our father had the son he always wanted. The house Duimpie had bought was old and in desperate need of repair and renovation. Duimpie was realistic enough to know that on a nursing salary he was never going to be able to afford a modern or newly renovated house despite some financial support from our father. He therefore both physically and psychologically rolled up his sleeves and set out to realize his vision of his perfect home by doing most of the renovations himself. Given the person that he was, with his artistic and refined temperament, nothing could be further from what he held dear. Fortunately, he had also inherited our father's will and determination, although he expressed it in very different ways. It was with grim determination that he started the renovations on his house. Of significant benefit to him was that he had at his disposal all the advice, support and equipment he needed to complete the renovations to his exacting standards. Our father was only too delighted to oblige and after many years of tension they finally found neutral ground where they both needed each other. It was during the years of renovating Duimpie's house that they established a truce and mutual respect that lasted until our father passed away.

It was as comical as it was admirable to observe my beloved brother acting in such a butch and alien way to his nature. With uncommon patience our father spent hours teaching Duimpie the basics of the building trade and, more importantly, how to use various potentially dangerous tools in a safe manner. At times this was a challenge, as Duimpie had no affinity with mechanical or technical equipment of any kind. On more than one occasion our father took a sledgehammer, or equivalently destructive tool, to a newly built wall or other attempt made by Duimpie, much to Duimpie's horror and frustration. The experience afforded our father endless entertainment, but also pride to observe how Duimpie developed the necessary skills to shape and renovate his home.

There were many tears, frustrated tantrums and outbreaks of swearing, not to mention injuries and aching muscles. It was a far cry from the artistic endeavors that occupied Duimpie's spare time, but he clung to the vision of what his home would look like once all the work was done. This sustained him through the years of frustration. Eventually, after all the laboring in the elements came to an end, he could once again give vent to his artistic abilities and focus on the interior design of his home. He was back in his natural habitat, but having persevered with the physical renovation of his house, it made the subsequent creative activities that much more rewarding and enjoyable. He had earned every moment of it. Apart from the satisfaction he gained from achieving something that was so alien to his nature, it also boosted his sense of self-worth enormously. Duimpie felt he could now truly hold his head high, knowing that he could do all the 'manly' things when needed and had now earned the right to say no to such macho activities in future.

Eventually, when his mother passed away, Pieter moved into Duimpie's home and together they carried out the final renovations and adjustments which suited them as a couple. Duimpie's home, whether it was a one bedroomed apartment or an enormous house, was his haven. At the end of a working day he would come home and, as he often said, pull up the drawbridge and immerse himself in the beauty, comfort and harmony of his home. Because his home meant so much to him, it was particularly poignant and heartbreaking when, towards the end of his life, he had to leave his haven and everything that meant so much to him. Until that time, however, he and Pieter settled into a peaceful existence as a couple, albeit within the constraints of a community that did not yet publicly recognize or acknowledge gay partnerships.

Their love and commitment to each other never waned, but continued to mature and deepen as the years went by. They were inseparable and did most things together. Pieter described his life with Duimpie as colorful; 'colorful and never a dull moment'. Not only did Duimpie love color, but also his personality was colorful and bright. It was rare to see him either down or moody, his enthusiasm for life just would not allow it. He needed very little sleep and would literally jump out of bed as soon as he woke up and throw open the curtains, often followed with his favorite saying: 'Open a new window, doll!' To him this meant that every day holds new experiences and adventures to be embraced wholeheartedly. Our mother was an eternal optimist and Duimpie had inherited the same trait by the bucket load.

Barry, the friend I referred to earlier, shared the memories of an exchange he witnessed between Duimpie and Pieter, just another example of the special nature of their relationship. It was on a summer's Sunday afternoon around midday. Anyone familiar with South African summers will know this is a particularly hot part of the day. Duimpie and I both inherited our father's fair coloring and we have always been conscious of avoiding too much direct sunlight. As Barry was a smoker they were sitting outside on the patio. It had a roof that could close to either keep off the rain or direct sun, but on this particular day the sun was shining from the side onto Duimpie's face. Duimpie didn't comment about the sun or make an attempt to move away, probably due to the fact that, as always, he was too engrossed in what his friends had to say. Without interrupting the conversation or making a fuss, Pieter got up and came back with the sun visor from the car and attached it to the awning in a way that shielded Duimpie from the sun.

According to Barry, the conversation never missed a beat. He reflected afterwards that it was one of the most loving and caring moments he had ever witnessed between two people. The significant act of kindness and consideration and Duimpie's simple 'thank you' was a moment that spoke more than any amount of words could ever do to convey the love and care for each other that they shared.

Duimpie's love of people was also accompanied by a strong sense of caring, so nursing was therefore the perfect profession for him. His patients adored him and, with his deep empathy for the suffering of others, he devoted himself wholeheartedly to them. Nothing was ever too much trouble and not only did he provide them with excellent nursing care, but he also showered them with his unbridled love and affection. He was passionate about what he saw the role and duty of a nurse to be, namely to provide the best nursing care possible to one's patients.

Although he learnt to distance himself to a certain extent from the pain and suffering of his patients, he was never immune to their plight and extended his love and support to include their families. He spent many hours comforting the families of dying patients, helping them through their darkest hours. Little did he know that the same fate would eventually await him. In many ways nursing as a profession is more than a job, it is a calling, and that was certainly the case for Duimpie. He cared for his patients on both a professional and a human level.

He had his fair share of personal insecurities and doubts, as was to be expected, but he had an underlying authority and an overall dedication to the profession that underpinned his nursing practice. He would not tolerate any deviation from the highest standards that he set for himself and his colleagues. These standards extended from the cleanliness of his wards to the comfort and care provided to the patients.

He was often conflicted over what he perceived to be the tension between the education of nursing and the actual practical, hands-on nursing care. As with any profession, nurses need an increasingly high level of education to meet the growing demands of the sophisticated science that accompanies nursing care. However, Duimpie's unwavering belief was that nursing care was first and foremost about caring for people during their time of need. He often became frustrated with younger members of staff, especially those gaining their nurse training through university, rather than the college and 'learning on the job' approach he had experienced.

Duimpie never let his staff and colleagues lose sight of the caring aspect of the profession, no matter how academically qualified they were. He was fond of saying that you didn't need a degree to provide a patient with a bedpan or to look after their general wellbeing and physical comfort. It is difficult to imagine many nursing staff remaining in the profession if they were driven by extrinsic rewards only. It must be one of the most stressful, demanding and poorly paid professions worldwide. Yet the intrinsic reward of making a difference to the lives of others is what helps nursing professionals cope with conditions most of us would have turned our backs on a long time ago.

Thankfully, the values of Florence Nightingale continue to inspire the nursing profession. Nursing is truly about service and this was a philosophy Duimpie lived at a personal as well as a professional level. He offered the same loyalty and dedication to his friends, family and strangers who might have been in need of help and support. He would happily and willingly nurse friends and family during their times of need. His passion for excellent nursing care never diminished irrespective of the seniority of his position as ward sister or as head of the day clinic he managed for a few years before he had to retire.

He never lost sight of the fact that his patients were multifaceted beings with complex and individual needs. He was ever conscious of the fact that the families of these patients placed explicit trust in him and his profession to care for their loved ones with the same respect and consideration he would want for himself and his own family. Alas, in his last months he was not afforded the same level of dedication and commitment to nursing care he showered on his own patients for all those years. Towards the end of his career he was deeply troubled and frustrated by what he perceived as the drop in standards of nursing care in South Africa. Unfortunately, it was representative of the erosion in standards at so many levels in South African society.

I shall pause to briefly introduce the challenges faced by South African society, which inevitably have a significant impact on the profession to which Duimpie was so committed. The nursing profession in South Africa has been in crisis for some time. Many of the challenges it faces are no doubt the same the world over, with some significant differences. Nursing in South Africa is one of many professions that have suffered from a steady hemorrhage of people leaving the country to seek a new life elsewhere. Thousands of nurses migrate each year searching for better pay, professional development, a better quality of life and above all personal safety. Health systems around the globe are heavily dependent on international recruitment, which exacerbates shortages in the countries from where nurses are recruited.

Often a better life and livelihood are at the root of decisions to migrate. Personal safety is a significant issue everyone faces on a daily basis in South Africa and safety is often quoted as one of the deciding factors to leave the country. Not many of us will quote personal safety as a contributing factor for changing our profession. The country experiences high levels of violent crime and nurses are exposed to the effects of violence in their personal as well as their professional lives. Some of the horror stories Duimpie told of the conditions of patients on admittance were disturbing to say the least. There is also a significant shortage of nurses, which results in heavy workloads for the remaining staff, excessive mandatory overtime and the unsatisfactory state of hospitals, which are without basic resources and equipment. Put together all of these factors and it makes it almost impossible for nurses to function effectively and maintain the standards to which Duimpie was always so committed.

On reflection, it is rather ironic that South Africa, with its history of the oppressive apartheid regime, has, since majority rule, failed to secure both the confidence and the respect for the rule of law. Instead, increased poverty and inequality have rocketed. The country's crime statistics make for horrific reading and have inevitably had serious consequences on the health system. Many of the laws that governed the country during apartheid were unjust, intended to entrench white domination, and it is true to say that these unfair laws were also often applied unfairly. Given its history there can be no argument that the apartheid state was deeply corrupt at all levels and individuals in positions of power were seldom held to account, nor were they brought before a court of law to account for acts of corruption and abuse of power.

It is therefore baffling that corruption and disrespect for the rule of law continue to be demonstrated by the regime that has followed the apartheid era. Those in political office appear to act with impunity, using the criminal justice system to avoid serious allegations of the abuse of power and misuse of state resources. The examples they set make it impossible for ordinary citizens to respect the law. Violence has become the norm and the country is widely lambasted as the rape and murder capital of the world. Not a statistic to be proud of. The reality of interpersonal violence is a daily occurrence for most people, and the poorer people are the more they are subjected to such violence. There is a yawning gap between rich and poor that under apartheid occurred by design. Since 1994 that gap has widened significantly and after the years of full democracy it must be one of the most unequal countries in the world.

Corruption is rife and any position in authority, especially those associated with politics or government, is seen as a gravy train that provides access to public funds. Overt bribery of officials is a regular occurrence and the cost of corruption has a devastating impact on the economy. Strikes are virtually a daily fact of life and a lack of investment in infrastructure has resulted in a serious decline in many services. At the time of writing, lack of investment and strike actions have left the power grids in a dangerous state of disrepair. The result is that 'lights out' is part of normal living, levying its own high price on the economy.

Given his temperament Duimpie yearned for a more peaceful and less threatening environment in which to spend his last few years. He and Pieter spent as much time with me in Europe as possible. Once again we had the opportunity to make wonderful memories, as Duimpie was fond of saying. It was very important to him to leave all of us with as many memories of happy times together as possible before his time was up. Once again, I will share with you some of the special memories we had the opportunity of creating after I had left South Africa.

CHAPTER NINE

How we treasured our times together during their trips to visit me in Europe. They were very different from the times we spent living together in South Africa, but they were equally as special. Duimpie and Pieter escaped South Africa as often as they could and on numerous occasions Pieter would insist on supporting Duimpie to come and visit on his own, thereby allowing him more opportunities to come to Europe. Pieter knew how much it meant to Duimpie not only to spend time in Europe, but for us to have time together.

It was such a far cry from their own environment where homes were surrounded by high walls protected by equally high-voltage fences and razor wires. Added to this was the ever-present fear of being hijacked while driving or attacked when you left your prison-like houses or offices. During their visits we would so often stop and marvel at the many sights Europe had to offer. Having spent years as kids dreaming about visiting Europe, here we were making it a reality and sometimes Duimpie wanted to pinch himself to make sure it wasn't merely a dream. We squeezed as much out of these experiences as we possibly could. When it was time to leave and return home, Duimpie would sob as though his heart was breaking. He longed to live in Europe, but it was never to be.

Duimpie and I could never get enough of the rich variety of architecture steeped in history that is around every corner in Europe. We also marveled at the stunning countryside; from the snow peaked mountains in Austria and Switzerland to the azure seas of the Mediterranean to the unspoilt beauty of the North East of England, my spiritual home. All of which were so very different from the South African scenery we were brought up with. Although South Africa has some beautiful mountain scenery and the luscious green and colorful Garden Route of the Cape, it also has miles of desert and grassland. It certainly has its own beauty, but it is mainly arid. The country can experience very dry periods during the summer months accompanied by high temperatures.

Duimpie always said it was a 'butch country for butch people' and we both favored the cooler European climate and its gentler, greener landscapes. It is interesting that Duimpie and I both had a fascination for the color green and its many shades and variations, especially those found in nature. Pieter remarked that Duimpie would always comment on the many shades of green as they drove on their various journeys around South Africa. Furthermore, it rubbed off on Pieter, and after Duimpie passed away, he would have 'conversations' with Duimpie about the many colors of green he continued to notice on his travels now without him.

My first 20 years or so living in England were spent mainly in the South East, including six years in Cambridgeshire and eight years in Oxfordshire; my homes being near the historic university cities of Cambridge and Oxford. The University of Cambridge was founded in 1209. However, modern day Cambridge is at the heart of the UK's high-tech industry. It is known as Silicon Fen, from the fens that surround the city and a play on Silicon Valley, its equivalent in the USA. The knowledge and research activities generated by the university resulted in startup businesses in software and biosciences that now successfully compete on an international level. Cambridge can proudly boast of housing one of the largest biomedical research clusters in the world.

Oxford is home to its equally famous university, the oldest in the English-speaking world. It was named as the 'city of dreaming spires' by the Victorian poet Matthew Arnold and is the gateway to what I believe is one of the most quintessential English counties, with its delightful Cotswold villages and chocolate box houses. In more modern times Oxford has become known as a city of two halves; the one half accommodating the ancient and historic buildings that constitute the university and the other half where mass production of cars was established in Cowley. Some of the most famous car manufacturers in the UK have been associated with Cowley, including the popular revived Mini manufactured by BMW.

On rare sunny English summer days Duimpie and I enjoyed nothing more than wandering around the striking old colleges that form the two universities. Our father instilled in us a love and respect for education and we were in awe of these two ancient seats of learning. A trip to either city wasn't complete without the occasional boat trip. Both Oxford and Cambridge are located next to rivers, resulting in a tradition of rowing. This in turn led to the tradition of the annual boat race between the two universities during the mid 1900s. It is usually held on the last weekend in March or the first weekend in April, on the Thames in west London. The race is a well-established and popular fixture in the British sporting calendar, watched by thousands from the riverbanks and millions more on TV worldwide.

Duimpie was also particularly fond of visiting Stratford-upon-Avon, the home of William Shakespeare. It is probably one of the most important tourist destinations in the UK and is equally steeped in history and culture. As with the two university cities, Stratford-upon-Avon nestles on the banks of a river. It is a unique representation of Olde England with its many ancient cottages, none more famous than the home of Anne Hathaway, the bride of William Shakespeare. Stratford is also home to the Royal Shakespeare Company, which produces plays by Shakespeare and his contemporaries as well as new works by living artists. Duimpie and I loved to explore the archetypal English village atmosphere and, much to the horror of my husband, would spend ages in the tourist shops, especially those offering arts and crafts.

With spirituality being important to Duimpie our visits to many of the European cathedrals always had a significant impact on him and we would spend numerous hours marveling at their awe-inspiring architecture. York Minster, the largest Gothic cathedral in Europe, was one of our favorites and we would take the time for quiet contemplation and reflection facilitated by its grandeur and tranquility. We paid a number of visits to the beautiful historic walled city of York in North Yorkshire. It has its own rich heritage providing a backdrop to many of the main political events that shaped the history of England.

In the heart of the old city is a collection of charming, narrow streets peppered with crooked half-timbered buildings. The most famous of these is known as the Shambles, one of the oldest and most picturesque streets in England. One can smell the history as one walks around admiring the many shops, selling everything from homemade sweets to antiques. As Europe's best preserved medieval street it is also its most visited one. It was impossible to drag Duimpie away from the many quirky shops of the Shambles as he was captivated by the variety of goods on display. As a visual person it was an irresistible offering of a palette consisting of many shapes, colors and designs.

During one of our trips around North Yorkshire, we visited Harrogate, the historic spa town located near the spectacular Yorkshire Dales. Around every corner are well-preserved examples of exquisite, historic architecture and immaculately maintained gardens. At the time of writing Harrogate was voted as one of the best places to live and declared as the third most romantic place in the world, beating places like Paris, which gives you a flavor of how special a place it is. I'm not sure I would agree with it topping Paris as a romantic destination, however. The Yorkshire accent, as delightful as it is, just doesn't quite have the same alluring quality of the French accent.

Our travels always included culinary delights of various kinds and Harrogate was no different. It is well known for its elegant tearooms and cafés spilling out onto the pavements, weather permitting. With Duimpie's sweet tooth a trip to one of these was a must. Probably the most prestigious of the tearooms is Betty's. It is internationally renowned as one of the most famous landmarks of Harrogate, established in 1919. During the summer months long queues of tourists patiently waiting for the famous afternoon tea experience remains a common sight.

With our Swiss roots we were always drawn to mountain regions and we particularly enjoyed visiting Austria, savoring the breathtaking mountain scenery to be found around every bend. During our last trip to Austria we spent a few days in Vienna, and as Duimpie is an opera aficionado, I treated them to an opera at the Wiener Staatsoper in celebration of his 50th birthday. As it was Vienna and they were lovers of Mozart, it had to be a Mozart evening. The Opera House is an exquisitely decorated building, which needed major rebuilding and renovation after being devastated by American bombing during the Second World War. It has since become one of the busiest and most important opera houses in the world. I was reminded of the other special birthday celebration at The Top of the Carlton many years before. Music has always featured highly in our lives, and whenever Duimpie visited me I made sure his visit included an opera, ballet or concert. This included a surprise trip for Pieter and Duimpie to the Royal Opera House in London's Covent Garden for a performance of the *Nutcracker* ballet. Nothing gave me greater pleasure than to enjoy Duimpie's childlike delight and enthusiasm for experiences such as these.

We could not leave Vienna without indulging in the traditional Austrian *Sachertorte*, which was a must given Duimpie's weakness for cake. It is the world's most famous chocolate cake and the only place to have it was in the café of the Sacher Hotel, opposite the Opera House and where the famous *Sachertorte* recipe was created. It continues to be made there from the same secret recipe handed down from generation to generation. The tradition of sitting in a café enjoying a freshly brewed coffee accompanied by a homemade cake or pastry was part of the culture we had created together since we were young. We had inherited a love of the café culture from our European ancestors and could spend hours watching the world go by over a cup of coffee.

Duimpie would always lament that such delicacies and simple delights were impossible to find in South Africa. I suspect the hot climate made it difficult to adorn pastries and cakes with lashings of cream and other perishable delights. To this day when I travel around and encounter especially lovely pâtisseries displaying their creative produce, I have to say, 'Duimpie would have loved this.' Before his death I would always email him photos of the mouthwatering delights I came across on my travels with the ubiquitous caption, 'Miss you and wish you were here.' I will always miss him and wish he were there to share such experiences with me.

As I'm writing, the beautiful and melancholic sounds of a violin playing the theme to *Schindler's List* enters my consciousness and it reminds me of one of our trips to Austria. Duimpie and Pieter were very keen to visit a concentration camp and we spent a day at Mauthausen-Gusen, a concentration camp near Linz in Upper Austria. Duimpie and Pieter were only too aware of the consequences of prejudice and the Holocaust was an extreme example of the behavior that results from such prejudice. The camp operated from 1938 to 1945 and in 1940 expanded considerably to become one of the largest labor camp complexes in German controlled Europe. The main camps were afforded a Grade III status, which meant they were as brutal and barbaric as they got and were reserved for those perceived, real or imagined, as the most severe political enemies of the Reich. It was given the nickname of *Knochenmühle*, which translates as bone-mill, and this is literally what it did, day after day.

The camps were used mainly for the extermination, through hard labor, of its prisoners labeled as the intelligentsia, educated people from the higher social classes of the countries invaded by the Nazis. The captives therefore included not only Jews but also gays of whom Hitler saw it as his duty to rid society. The aim was to work inmates in the quarries until they were physically unable to continue. At that stage they were sent to the gas chambers on site. The treatment of the prisoners was beyond comprehension and it moved us deeply as we read the accounts and watched the video footage displayed in the museum. We came across a memorial in the form of a wooden cross near the entrance to the complex that was made from rough and ragged pieces of wood. Duimpie was so moved by it that, when he returned home, he had a gold crucifix made to resemble the memorial that he always wore on a chain around his neck. To him it was a stark reminder of the ultimate prejudice.

CHAPTER TEN

Nowhere in Europe are my memories of times spent with Duimpie as special as the ones we shared in the North East of England where I finally settled. A large part of my career meant I worked and traveled internationally. While working in Israel, I was approached by the Dean of one of the business schools in the North East to join them as an academic, which I accepted. So started my career as an academic and consultant. My husband, my partner at that time, found me a beautiful old Victorian town house, which I immediately fell in love with and made an offer on as soon as I saw it. The views from my windows are breathtaking with miles of immaculately kept parks and the sea beyond as backdrop.

There are miles of golden sands and, if we had regular sunny weather in England, it would no doubt be a very popular holiday destination. However, the result might mean the loss of the unspoilt beauty of the region. Not many people can boast of watching ships sail past their bedroom windows. The first time

Duimpie experienced the sound of a ship's horn before its departure from the port, he insisted on racing to the harbor to see the departing ship in person. He had a knack of inventing quirky sayings and he couldn't get over the 'honking' of the ship as it left. To this day Laurence and I comment on the 'honking' of the ship whenever we hear a particularly good example of a loud ship's horn when leaving the harbor.

One of the first places we visited from my home in the North East was the beautiful Lake District in the North West of England. It is also known as the Lakes or Lakeland, a mountainous region with numerous lakes both large and small. It is particularly popular with hill walkers and climbers as well as anyone seeking the tranquility offered by its beauty, with a wide range of hotels and bed and breakfasts dotted on the shores of the lakes and in the countryside. Duimpie was overwhelmed by the peace and tranquility of the Lakes. Coming from urban South Africa and its difficult living conditions, he was unaccustomed to the fact that he could walk around in the countryside and towns without any fear for his personal safety. He did, however, once baffle the local police in Keswick when he decided to go for a walk at five o'clock in the morning.

As a person who needed very little sleep, he would often be up and about long before sunrise. He always woke up with the enthusiasm and optimism of a child and could not wait for me to get up at a more civilized hour. This he did regularly, much to my disgust, when we lived together. He would breeze into my room on a weekend at 6:30 if I was lucky, throwing open the curtains and singing at the top of his voice, 'Rise and shine, it's a bbbbeeeaaauuutttiiifffuull day, doll!' By this time he had scrubbed every inch of the apartment until it sparkled, washing was on the line and he was probably on his second pot of filter coffee. Unlike him I needed my beauty sleep, but it was not to be as his excitement for what the day may hold meant sleep was not an option for me. When in Europe he wanted to savor every moment of the freedom from the constraints forced on him by the threat of personal violence in South Africa.

On this particular morning in the Lakes, he decided to don sweater and cap and go for a walk. Even in the summer the early mornings in England, and especially in the mountains, are fresh and often shrouded in mist. This, of course, has its own charm and beauty especially for someone from a hot climate who wakes up to bright sunshine every day. I often remember with amusement a line in the film *White Mischief*: 'Not another fucking beautiful day', which I think aptly describes life in a hot climate. Many of my English friends are incapable of comprehending that constant hot weather and wall-to-wall sunshine can become as monotonous as the ever-present rain and grey skies of England.

I digress, back to the early, misty morning in the Lakes. Not many people decide to go for a walk at that time of the morning and, with his experience of police motivations and their less than diplomatic approach, he nearly collapsed when stopped by the local police patrol car. He found it almost impossible to answer their questions through his chattering teeth, not from the cold but the fear of being stopped. As it turned out, they were merely concerned that he might have been a lost tourist after a night out and offered him a lift back to the cottage where we were staying.

As soon as Duimpie arrived at my home in the North East, he would first enjoy a long walk on the stretches of beaches and parks opposite my house, irrespective of the weather. The North East of England is particularly well known for the rich natural beauty of its coastline. It is also an area of historical significance with numerous ancient castles dotted along the coast, all bearing testimony to the importance of the region in contributing to the history and defence of the UK. Duimpie loved the fresh air and, more importantly, the freedom to wander and explore at his leisure without constantly looking over his shoulder and tightly clutching his bag by his side.

Probably another reason for the attraction the region had for Duimpie was its strong religious history. The most famous of the monasteries and abbeys to be found in the region is the Holy Island of Lindisfarne, a tidal island close to the border with Scotland. Holy Island, as it is also known, is accessible via a causeway during low tides and is a haven for those seeking peace and seclusion. Then there is the famous Durham Cathedral presiding over the historic Durham city from its vantage position on a rocky promontory next to the castle. Durham is also home to another university, which, like Cambridge and Oxford, can trace its roots back into the annals of history. While writing I reflect how I have been attracted to living in or near university cities.

As a result of the Industrial Revolution, iron and steel, coal mining and shipbuilding dominated the economy of the North East. The region's proud and majestic bridges are a legacy of its contribution to engineering and industry. One such bridge is the gondola transporter bridge in Middlesbrough, which is one of the longest transporter bridges in the world. It is also one of the few to have survived. After a lifespan of 103 years, it recently received a major overhaul and continues to provide a regular service to public transport wanting to cross the River Tees. In addition to these heavy industries, glass manufacturing played a key role in the regional economy. Stained glass glaziers have worked on Wearmouth and Jarrow monasteries from as early as AD 674. During the 19th century the region made a significant contribution to the supply of glass throughout the rest of the UK.

Anyone remotely familiar with the North East will know that shipbuilding was one of the main industries in the region. Ships have been built here since as early as the 1300s. Due to its significant maritime history it is perhaps therefore not surprising that the region was home to one of the most famous sailors of all time, Captain James Cook, who sailed his ship, the HM Bark *Endeavour*, from Whitby. The journey resulted in Captain Cook discovering and naming the antipodean continents and islands as well as many islands in the Pacific Ocean.

Just as rugby is followed with a quasi religious fervor in South Africa, so is football in the North East of England. One could argue, possibly more so. The identity of the region is inextricably linked with that of football. It is so much more than recreation; it is a way of life. Given the lack of success of the football clubs in the region, the stoic loyalty and enthusiasm of the fans are to be admired. It is an enthusiasm that one could say borders on fanaticism. It was a novel experience for me to observe how much of daily life is organized around football due to the traffic holdups following home matches and the inconceivable thought of missing a match. Having had the opportunity to attend a couple of matches in Newcastle courtesy of two of my clients, I am still trying to understand what the attraction is all about, and probably never will.

Historically, the North East has always been seen as the poor cousin of the South of England and a significant proportion of the UK population has a limited and prejudiced knowledge of the North East. It is probably one of the best-guarded secrets of the UK and I have come to the conclusion that the region conspires with the myth held by the rest of the British population. Understandably, they do not want to be invaded by Southerners buying up houses for weekend and holiday homes, which would inevitably result in pricing the local population out of the market. Foreigners have an even greater lack of knowledge of the North East. The region is mainly associated with football, the annual marathon – the Great North Run – and, in recent times, television programs that, although they are of the quality expected of British dramas, I do not think necessarily portray the region at its best. This reinforces the prejudiced view held of the North East by Southerners.

As a region it has a strong community spirit, which has become a rarity in other parts of the UK. A contributing factor to the erosion of community spirit elsewhere, particularly in the South of England, is the migration of people for career opportunities and the tradition of commuting to work. If one spends two to three hours a day commuting, there isn't the bond with the community where one lives, nor the time to develop such an attachment. In addition, further relocation is always a possibility for commuters. Apart from the natural beauty of the North East region, it is less populated and therefore doesn't suffer from the same frustrations as the South East, such as traffic congestion and overcrowding. For whatever reason, Northeasterners live up to their reputation of being much more friendly and welcoming than their Southern cousins. All of these independent factors make for a high quality of life and understandably therefore the people of the region do not want to broadcast this fact too loudly.

One of the things the region is famous for is its Geordie accent, voted as one of the sexiest accents in the UK. It doesn't, however, mean you necessarily understand what Geordies are saying. One of the more earthy phrases of the local parlance that intrigued Duimpie was the colorful way of saying fuck off. His fascination was not only with the way it was pronounced but the frequency with which it popped up in normal conversation in certain social circles. It sounded something like *fook orf*. We went to see the film *Billy Elliot*, set in County Durham, and when Billy asks his friend Tony, 'Do you ever think about death?', Tony replies, 'Fook orf.' Duimpie roared with laughter; having heard it so many times over the previous few weeks, it affirmed his experience of the phrase as part of the local dialect and expression.

My husband Laurence, being of a creative and artistic nature, decided to create two posters, one with the word *fook* on it and the other with the word *orf*.

When the particular holiday Duimpie and Pieter had spent with us came to an end, my husband and I bade them farewell at Newcastle airport, holding up the two posters wishing them *FOOK ORF!* I did not think that Duimpie would be in any way capable of getting onto the plane as he was simply hysterical with laughter. I seriously considered calling for a wheelchair to transport him to their waiting plane. The four of us created entertainment for fellow passengers that I doubt the airport had seen the likes of before or since. I felt like a celebrity surrounded by flashing cameras and crowds, all wanting to see what the merriment was about. It was one of those memories Duimpie and I referred to time and time again when we were reminiscing about the times we had shared together. Its recollection always had the ability to evoke fresh fits of laughter in us. Before their visits, my husband would record many of the Graham Norton chat shows. Duimpie adored Graham Norton and his somewhat risqué shows in the earlier days with strong adult humor. It was nothing like the programs they could watch on South African television.

Duimpie and Pieter spent a few Christmas holidays with us and it was during their last Christmas visit that I noticed Duimpie becoming unusually quiet and subdued towards the end of their trip. I attributed it to the fact that their impending departure saddened him as it always did. However, looking back I can see that it was the beginning of his six-year ordeal with cancer. He mentioned in passing, when I asked him whether he was OK, that he had backache and would go and see the doctor when he got home. I didn't pay much attention to this fact as nurses notoriously suffer from back problems. It is an occupational hazard. I was therefore not overly alarmed and we had our usual sad separation at the airport when they left.

CHAPTER ELEVEN

Shortly after Christmas my husband and I went to our house in France and it was there that I got the call from Duimpie that changed all our lives forever. As soon as I heard his voice I knew something was drastically wrong. It was clear from his tone that the worst possible had happened. Various scenarios raced through my mind at lightning speed. At first I thought our mother had been taken seriously ill or something had happened to my sister or her two boys. Nothing could have prepared me for the news he was about to reveal.

He started by saying, 'There is no easy way to say this so I will just say it. I have terminal prostate cancer with five years maximum to live.' Then silence. We remained silent for what seemed an eternity and the only thing I could say over and over was, 'I don't believe it, how? Why? It cannot be possible, surely!' I kept thinking that I was having a nightmare and that I would wake up with a jolt, relieved that it was only a dream. Eventually the reality started to sink in and

Duimpie explained what had transpired since they returned home after Christmas. We kept going over the same things and eventually ended up crying together for ages. I so wished I could be there with him just to hug and comfort him. During times like these I had to live with the consequences of being far away from my loved ones.

Our father had died of prostate cancer approximately five years before. The difference was that he was in his late seventies and Duimpie was only in his early fifties with so much life still to live and dreams to realize. He had always known that he had a very good chance of inheriting the prostate cancer gene and because of this he regularly went for checkups. With his medical knowledge he knew that early diagnosis is critical in the treatment of any cancer. All tests had always come back with negative results. It was the fact that he had always been given the all clear that made it so difficult to comprehend. How could he possibly go from a clean bill of health one day all the way through to terminal cancer only months after? It was simply inconceivable.

As soon as they had returned to South Africa he went for all the relevant tests to determine what was causing the backache, and the rectal bleeding he had experienced while with me but which he did not want to mention so as not to spoil the Christmas holiday for anyone. These tests also included a Prostate-Specific Antigen (PSA) test that detects whether there are any cancer markers present. The PSA test determines the level of a protein that is produced by the prostate gland. The higher the level the more likely it is that a man has prostate cancer. It is also carried out during various subsequent cancer treatments to determine whether the cancer is responding to the treatment and, if so, how well.

The oncologist whom Duimpie consulted was a colleague and, given that they were in the same profession, there was more honesty and no holds barred discussion than he might have had with another patient. During the few days of waiting for the results Duimpie moved around like a sleepwalker, struggling to focus on day-to-day activities and coping with the demands of his job. I'm not sure whether his medical knowledge was a good thing or not. The downside was that he could anticipate the worst case scenario. He and Pieter would just sit for long periods without saying anything, just holding hands and silently offering support and courage to each other. Both trying to convince themselves and each other that the results would be fine and medication would help Duimpie with whatever back problems he had developed. After all, he was a nurse and back problems were part of the job.

The day came for the results of the blood tests and Duimpie went in to see the oncologist on his own with Pieter tensely staying behind in the waiting area. This was still during the time when gay partners were not considered the next of kin. The oncologist came straight to the point and told Duimpie, 'Your blood tests show outrageously high levels of PSA and I suggest we carry out a digital rectal examination before deciding on the next steps.' Given the high level of Duimpie's PSA test, there was no doubt that he had prostate cancer. With that one sentence Duimpie had the carpet ripped from under him and all he could do was sit and stare at the oncologist without moving. His years in the medical profession and dealing with patients in a similar position did not prepare him for the day when he would be in that position himself. Now he was the patient being told that he had cancer.

After the physical examination the oncologist stated that the size and texture of his prostate gave cause for concern. The next stage was to carry out a biopsy, followed by an MRI scan to determine whether the cancer had spread and, if so, how far it had spread. They would then be in a position to discuss the most appropriate plan of treatment. Finally Duimpie found his voice and in a tone bordering on hysteria and filled with disbelief he almost shouted, 'But I regularly came to you for tests and they always came back negative! You told me to go away and come back in a year or so. What went wrong?'

The oncologist understood only too well the emotional and psychological upheaval Duimpie was going through and offered both support as well as practical suggestions for moving to the next stage. He would book Duimpie in for the necessary biopsy, followed by a scan if necessary. It was as if some invisible hand had all of a sudden turned on a clock, ticking away the minutes, days and months, and who knew how long it would be before it finally stopped. Who will determine when it stops and will they know in advance? These were just some of the myriad questions buzzing through Duimpie's mind like a swarm of angry bees.

When Pieter saw Duimpie come out of the consulting room he immediately knew what the results were by the expression of total shock on his face. Without saying a word, he took Duimpie by the arm and they made their way to the car in silence. It was only when they got to the privacy of their own home that they both broke down. They sobbed and clung to each other like victims of a shipwreck cast asunder in stormy seas. For days they just went over the same things, trying to understand why the cancer had not showed up on any previous tests. Then came the hope that the cancer had not spread beyond the prostate and therefore there was still the opportunity to contain it. Thus began what Duimpie termed 'the rollercoaster ride'. One minute you are up and hopeful that the next lot of treatment will be the cure, only to have your hopes shattered by new results, plunging you back into despair. Interestingly, a number of other prostate cancer patients who shared their stories with me used the same analogy. Duimpie's philosophy was always to take one step at a time and to live in the moment and from there on in this became his daily mantra.

In the weeks following Duimpie's diagnosis he and Pieter would often wake up in the middle of the night and Pieter would make them a cup of coffee or tea and they would just sit and talk, trying to make sense of it all. They would reminisce about their life together and the special moments and experiences they had enjoyed or they would hold each other and cry at the unfairness of it all. All their dreams and plans for their retirement were in shreds and instead replaced with an empty void of darkness and despair. It was difficult to imagine that they could become even closer than they had always been. However, it put everything into perspective and the time they had left became their moment-by-moment, day-by-day focus.

Pieter mused in almost disbelief how ordinary their lives had been up until then. 'So ordinary,' Pieter remarked to me on one occasion. 'None of what one might associate with a gay couple; nightlife and living it up as with some of our friends, or even promiscuous living. Why us?' A question every cancer patient and their family will ask at some stage on their journey. When we were young and living together I had to drag him out to engage in some social life, as he was just so careful and worried about doing something 'wrong' and putting himself at risk.

Quality time was always so important to Duimpie and it became even more so. He and Pieter were determined to fill every moment with whatever was important to them, stripping away superfluous activities and the 'have to', 'must do, 'can't possibly do', dutiful actions and pursuits we all engage in. This included not wasting their time with people who didn't want to make the effort of contributing to the friendship and only wanted to take. How trivial we can all be at times and almost flippantly offer empty words like 'we must get together', knowing full well that we won't. It then becomes even more banal and empty knowing that you literally only had a few years left to live with very little time to 'get together'.

It is also a time when friendships are put to the test and, as is often the case, some people stopped calling. One reason is possibly that people don't know what to say or how to say it. It seems totally inappropriate to ask someone with terminal cancer, 'How are you?' How does one behave with and around someone in Duimpie's position? However, the friends who mattered and supported them through their ordeal were the ones who understood it was not necessary to say anything at all, but just to be there with love and hugs when things were bad and humor and laughter where possible.

Duimpie set out to befriend what he had termed 'the old monster'. Instead of resisting and fighting it every step of the way, trying to exorcise it from his body, he learnt to tune into his body and the messages it conveyed to him. If he was in pain he would take it easy and have a rest without pushing himself to continue with whatever activity or person he was engaged with. He learnt that this paid off in the long run and helped him to manage 'the old monster' as best he could, with the many drugs and treatments he went through. Little by little, or step by step in his words, he came to terms with the inevitable and, in his naturally optimistic way, made the most of the life he had left.

CHAPTER TWELVE

After his initial diagnosis and blood tests that returned a PSA in excess of 1000, the oncologist suggested they start with hormone therapy to try to starve the tumor of the testosterone that the cancer needed to grow. At this stage, however, it was unclear as to how aggressive the cancer was and whether it had spread beyond the prostate area. Prostate cancer is a complex disease and research suggests there are numerous different types. It is also difficult to know at the time of diagnosis how the particular cancer of an individual patient will respond to different treatments.

As any cancer patient will know, the side effects of any of the treatments can range from mild to severe, adding an additional element to the rollercoaster ride. Days after his hormone therapy treatment began fatigue set in for Duimpie. Although he had the medical knowledge of what to expect, it was nevertheless a challenge to deal with the side effects. He was first and foremost a patient and not the medical expert. Apart from the fatigue, Duimpie also developed hot flushes and gained weight. Duimpie saw the funny side of experiencing symptoms akin to menopause and said, 'This is the closest I will probably get to know what it feels like to be a woman!'

He was always slim despite his sweet tooth and he found it difficult to deal with the weight gain, particularly in a hot climate and coupled with hot flushes. Furthermore, he also experienced mood swings, but it was difficult to know whether it was due to the hormone treatment or the natural emotional response in dealing with the challenges of coping with terminal cancer. The calm and practical approach with which Pieter dealt with the crisis was the best way to help Duimpie cope with the emotional disruption caused by the treatment. Initially the hormone therapy reduced Duimpie's PSA count and he and Pieter once again became hopeful that it would either slow down or stop the cancer from growing and spreading. However, the reprieve was short lived and further PSA tests, a few weeks later, confirmed that the cancer markers had begun to increase again.

The oncologist suggested that a biopsy would give them a clearer indication as to the nature of the cancer and therefore help to determine the next steps. The sample from the biopsy was sent away for tests. Once again the results did not offer any hope and showed that his particular cancer was very aggressive. The biopsy had produced a Gleason grade of $4 + 5 = 9$. The Gleason grade allows the oncologist to determine how aggressive the cancer is and how likely it is to spread outside the prostate area. Cancer cells have different patterns that are determined by the speed with which the cells are likely to grow and spread.

The cancer pattern is normally given a grading from 1 to 5 and known as the Gleason grade. If the cells are cancerous they will be given a grading above 3 and if the grading is below 3 it means that cancer is probably not present. It is possible that there is more than one grade of cancer in the samples taken through a biopsy. The overall Gleason grade is then determined by adding these two Gleason grades; the first grade being the most common of the samples and the second the highest of the remainder. The higher the score the more likely it is that the cancer will spread, and in Duimpie's case it was probably as high as it could get.

At this stage the oncologist discussed with Duimpie the possibility of a radical prostatectomy, which meant removing the prostate altogether. The advantage was that if the cancer had not spread, chances are that it could be removed completely. If the PSA markers dropped after the surgery, it would be an indication of the success of the surgery. On the other hand, the disadvantages are urinary and erectile problems that would probably result from the surgery. Furthermore, if the cancer had spread, the surgeon may not be able to remove all of it. Duimpie and Pieter agonized for days as to what the best course of action was, taking into account the irreversible consequences for both Duimpie's health as well as their relationship. In the end, they both decided that whatever the consequences of such radical surgery may be, it was worth it if it meant the cancer could be removed or at least contained. They finally made the decision to go ahead and the oncologist made the necessary arrangements for surgery.

Apart from all of the physical and mental agony and emotions they were experiencing in coming to terms with the fact that they had limited time together, they had to continue the charade of being nothing more than good friends in public. At times it was a source of great sadness and even anger. Neither of them would ever have behaved in a way that would flaunt their sexual orientation or alienate others, but there are times when the physical display of support and love goes a long way in providing a partner with comfort. Unlike other couples who could draw strength from each other, the comfort of having your partner with you, holding your hand before surgery and being there for you when you came around, was not possible for them. In their deepest despair they had to continue with the public censorship of their relationship. It was not possible for Pieter to be recognized as Duimpie's next of kin and he did not have the same rights and expectations as a heterosexual partner when accompanying Duimpie to his treatments or when he consulted with the various medical professionals. Fortunately, as Duimpie knew his medical team very well as colleagues, some of these rules were ignored.

The surgery itself went well and Duimpie recovered fairly quickly. Further tests offered some hope as Duimpie's PSA markers had dropped significantly. However, not long after the surgery Duimpie began once again to suffer from severe back and hip pain and he had to take high dosages of pain relief. The back and hip pain raised the suspicion of the oncologist that the cancer had already spread into his bones and to confirm this he arranged for Duimpie to undergo an MRI as well as a bone scan. As was expected the cancer had spread.

Given the fact that the cancer had made its way into the bones around the pelvis area, chemotherapy was the next step in his treatment regime. This was in addition to the hormone therapy. The theory is that chemotherapy, which uses anti-cancer drugs, will kill the prostate cancer cells wherever they are in the body. Furthermore, chemotherapy is expected to shrink and slow down the growth of cancer. Apart from prolonging life it is also helpful in controlling or delaying symptoms such as pain. Again Duimpie and Pieter's hopes were raised that the chemotherapy would contain the further spreading of the cancer. As with any drug or medication, there are numerous side effects and these vary from patient to patient. One of the common symptoms of chemotherapy is fatigue and often also severe constipation. Duimpie suffered all of the expected side effects as well as a few additional ones given his history as a premature baby that had left a legacy of weaknesses in his body.

It was hard to believe that two years had passed since that fateful Christmas that heralded a change in all of our lives. Pieter reflected on how their conversations and daily routines had become dominated by the presence of cancer. It affected so many decisions they made and it was an ever-present companion, albeit an uninvited one. It had gatecrashed their lives and turned them upside down and inside out. Given the level of Duimpie's pain and the side effects of the different treatments he was undergoing, the oncologist strongly recommended that Duimpie retire from his career as a Day Clinic Manager in a private hospital. He was finding it very challenging to cope with the day-to-day strains and, although the hospital management and his colleagues were very understanding and supportive when he needed time off for treatment and recovery, it was becoming nigh on impossible for him to continue.

Before his diagnosis Duimpie had become increasingly frustrated with what he perceived as the drop, or total absence, of the nursing standards he had held so dear throughout his career. It was therefore a relief on the one hand to put all that behind him and to focus on looking after himself and spending as much time as possible with Pieter, the family and their close friends. It made a significant difference as he could now look after himself much more carefully, with the psychological benefit of the absence of daily work pressures.

His medical knowledge was a mixed blessing. He had lived with and around illness and death for many years, but when you are the patient death is no longer an abstraction but an omnipresent reality. From the outset Duimpie chose to be as open as possible with all of us about the details of his illness, treatments and the advantages and disadvantages that would inevitably follow. Although his openness about his cancer brought the reality of the seriousness of his illness into stark reality, I think it made us all better equipped to deal with the constant and unexpected surprises the 'old monster' seemed to relish in producing. It also helped us individually to deal with our own emotional trauma, but more importantly, we were better able to provide support to Duimpie and Pieter.

Given his natural tendency to look after others first and foremost, he took great pains in making contingencies for our mother's care when he wouldn't be there any more. It was heartbreaking to all of us to observe our mother's suffering at the thought of losing her second son. A parent should not bury their children and to have to bury both sons is beyond comprehension. I believe the resilient and naturally optimistic disposition of our mother was the only thing that gave her the strength to face the inevitable.

Duimpie's retirement meant that he was able to spend much more time with our mother and, despite the circumstances, they also had a lot of fun together. No matter how dire the situation, laughter was never far away from either of them. They would often go out shopping together, go to the cinema, visit friends and regularly play a simple board game they had discovered. Despite its simplicity it afforded them hours of entertainment, not to mention fits of hysterical laughter. They always had a knack of seeing the funny side of everything, often resulting in bouts of uncontrollable laughter. They shared the same sense of humor and would often leave the rest of the family at a loss as to what they found so funny. If laughter is the best medicine, as it is often claimed to be, they both had an overdose of it. Duimpie was determined for all of us to 'make as many memories as possible' in his words, and to bank these for the times ahead when he would no longer be with us.

CHAPTER THIRTEEN

One of Duimpie's deepest concerns was to ensure that, when he was no longer there, Pieter was taken care of, especially as he would not be recognized as the legitimate surviving spouse or partner. They had experienced much horror in their lives with gay friends who had lost everything due to the fact that gay partners did not have the same rights as heterosexual couples, despite the fact that, in some cases, there existed legal wills. Amazing how people react when money is involved and relatives who had ostracized their gay family members all of a sudden crawled out of the woodwork to claim whatever money, property and possessions were up for grabs. Duimpie was determined to do whatever it took to prevent such a fate befalling Pieter. Every family has their rogue members who could possibly carry out such despicable deeds.

Ina, a brilliant lawyer and a friend of theirs, spent much time in drawing up legal contracts to prevent such a thing from happening to Pieter. During this process, the South African Parliament voted for a bill allowing same-sex civil marriage. For Duimpie and Pieter it was the most precious gift anyone could have bestowed on them. At last it meant that Pieter would legally be recognized as Duimpie's next of kin and be afforded the same rights and protection as any other person in a legally binding relationship. Just how much of a benefit this would be only became clear later on. It meant that Pieter now had the right to make joint decisions regarding Duimpie's healthcare or on his behalf if he was unable to do so. Furthermore, Pieter now had the right, as his partner, to benefit from the private health scheme Duimpie had access to through his work. These were just some of the many benefits they could now enjoy as a married couple. More importantly, they now legitimately had the right to publicly announce and celebrate their commitment to each other. They were ecstatic and wasted no time in arranging their civil marriage.

One of their favorite destinations for a holiday or just a long weekend break was a place called Clarens, known as the jewel of the province called the Free State in South Africa. It is located in the eastern part of the province and approximately three hours' drive from Johannesburg. Clarens nestles in the beautiful sandstone Rooiberg Mountains. From there the Maluti mountain range further on is visible in its beautiful hues of blues and purples. Although mild, the climate gets cold enough in the winter for snow. However, in the summer it offers the holidaymaker the sun foreign travelers would expect of South Africa. It is a paradise for outdoor lovers with all the usual activities that go along with outdoor pursuits.

Clarens is a destination on the scenic Highland Route with the well-known and popular Golden Gate National Park nearby. Apart from its tranquil ambiance, one of the attractions Clarens held for Duimpie and Pieter was that it is a haven for well-known artists who either live there or visit regularly. The result is an Aladdin's cave of art galleries impossible for Duimpie to resist. Needless to say they spent many hours wandering through the galleries and, in Duimpie's words, 'gorged on food for the soul'.

Their civil marriage was a very quiet affair and only two couples from their closest friends joined them for the ceremony in Clarens. Once the legal side of the service was conducted, they went a few miles to a favorite spot of Duimpie and Pieter's in the mountains, which they had always visited when staying in Clarens. One of their friends was an ordained Dutch Reformed Minister and, as a spiritual person, it was very important for Duimpie to have a spiritual element to their proceedings. Trevor the Minister and his partner Gerrie were close friends of Duimpie and Pieter's. Gerrie had become part of the family over the years when he was growing up. Gerrie was the son of a close colleague and friend of Duimpie, so they had known him from a very young age and often offered support to him as a young man growing up gay in a conservative community. In fact, Duimpie and Pieter always referred to Gerrie as their 'daughter'. I cannot help but muse that many of the staunch and conservative *Dominies* (Afrikaans for Dutch Reformed Church Ministers) would have turned in their graves at an ordained Minister conducting a same-sex civil marriage ceremony. How times have changed!

I was reminded of another Dutch Reformed Minister who had played a significant part in our family history, albeit briefly. We were brought up in the Dutch Reformed faith and, as is expected of good members of the congregation, we regularly attended Sunday church services, followed by Sunday School and were eventually confirmed at the appropriate age. During the time my eldest brother Charles was training to be a pilot, we had a young, newly appointed Minister whom our father became very fond of. Not many people had the ability to impress our father, but this particular Minister did. He was charismatic and there was no doubt in the sincerity of his faith and his desire to serve his church and the community.

When Charles died, it was he who conducted a very moving service as part of Charles' military funeral. Our father would often reflect on the service and reminisce that he would have loved to know what had happened to this particular Minister. We had moved away by this time and my parents had lost touch with him. It just so happened that a number of years later Duimpie and I went to a gathering at the home of some of our gay friends and who should walk in but the Minister in question. Duimpie and I looked at each other in total disbelief and to say that we were speechless would have been an understatement. What on earth was a Dutch Reformed Minister doing partying with a group of gay men? We were unable to fathom it out and we had to contain ourselves not to approach him and start interrogating him with a barrage of questions.

I was very young when Charles died, but the Minister, or should I say at this stage, ex-Minister, recognized Duimpie and came over to talk to us. He was as charming as I remembered him and his story was equally a sad one, bearing testament to the prejudice and narrow-mindedness of the Afrikaans community at that time. Like so many other gay people of his age, he had fought and suppressed his homosexuality until he could no longer do so. Religion obviously played a big role not only in his suppression of his sexuality, but also ultimately in his decision to come out. Of course, it meant his career as a Dutch Reformed Minister, and probably a member of any Dutch Reformed congregation, was over. Like Duimpie, he had married, but unlike Duimpie, he had children and cruelly he was prevented from seeing his children after he publicly announced that he was homosexual. He had certainly paid a high price for challenging the bigotry that permeated the mainly dominant white Afrikaans culture of the Dutch Reformed communities.

I was so often tempted to share his story with our father. I thought it might go some way in helping him to recognize that being a gay man was not a lifestyle choice, nor a disease, and that many gay people had suffered greatly as a result of rejection from their families and communities. In the end, Duimpie and I decided that it would serve no purpose other than potentially cause our father pain and possibly tarnish the memories he had of Charles and his burial service.

Now, at last Duimpie could put away the worries he had about what would happen to Pieter after he had gone. He could focus on the continuous journey of treatments and coping with the inevitable side effects. Similar to Duimpie's own experiences, a fellow prostate cancer patient told me of his frustrations and anger at what he perceived as the insensitivities and idiocy of those who had no insight or concept of what it meant to be a cancer patient. All of a sudden everyone you know has an off-the-wall miracle cure ranging from alternative medicines and therapies to more ludicrous beliefs of how the power of positive thinking alone will cure you of your cancer.

It was no different for Duimpie and as a medically trained practitioner he got really angry with some of the more bizarre quackery suggested to him. I have no doubt that the motivations of friends were well meaning and I confess that I was just as guilty as the rest. I was so desperate to try to find a cure and wanted him to try anything, just in case. I spent hours on the Internet in an attempt to find research which may be pioneering, in its early stages and therefore not yet known by mainstream medicine. I kept thinking that in a few years they will discover a cure for prostate cancer, but it will be too late for Duimpie. If we can only keep him alive until then, he could benefit from that miracle that was just waiting to be discovered. Fortunately, Duimpie had enough insight to understand my despair and he also had the medical experience to take the advice naïvely offered by others and myself for what it was.

On a lighter and humorous note, a friend of theirs wanted to offer his own miracle cure for Duimpie and Barry suggested cannabis. For many years he had suffered from the most excruciating back and leg pain as the result of an incurable disease and an operation that went horribly wrong. It had left Barry unable to walk without the support of leg braces and crutches. He was in constant pain and had found that, on occasion, cannabis helped with his pain management. He finally succeeded in persuading Duimpie to at least give it a try and see whether it had any impact on his own pain levels. He made arrangements to visit Duimpie and Pieter on a particular evening, armed with the necessary amount of cannabis that was to be brewed as a tea. Halfway on his journey to Duimpie and Pieter he was confronted by flashing blue lights and a police roadblock that meant every car was being stopped for questioning. Barry's life flashed before his eyes and his natural fear and response to blue lights as a gay man made it almost impossible for him to drive. Added to this was the knowledge that he was in possession of cannabis, which, as in many other countries, was illegal at the time.

In South Africa, with its high level of drug and other crime related activities, if Barry had stopped to think about it logically, the small amount of cannabis he had on him would most certainly not have interested the police. However, all he could focus on was his fear of the police and being on the wrong side of the law. It was too late to turn around without causing any suspicion and he just had to crawl closer to the blockade. Eventually it was his turn and a torchlight was flashed in his face and questions fired at him. It finally penetrated his paralyzed and fear induced brain that the police were looking for suspects in a gang robbery that had resulted in a murder. He clearly had no information to share and the police waved him through.

When he finally arrived at Duimpie and Pieter's house they had to physically help him out of the car. Cannabis was not enough for Barry that night and it took a stiff brandy before the color finally returned to his face and, albeit stuttering uncontrollably, he relayed his experience to Duimpie and Pieter. They saw the funny side of it and eventually Barry joined in with his own laughter bordering on hysteria. Duimpie never got to try the cannabis, but the event certainly afforded them with much entertainment for a long while afterwards. Needless to say, as the story was retold it got a bit taller every time. Sadly, during the time of writing, Barry finally lost a long battle with his own health problems and he died unexpectedly.

CHAPTER FOURTEEN

As part of his ongoing treatment, the doctor recommended Duimpie undergo surgery to remove lymph nodes that had become affected by the cancer. Added to this was the removal of lymph nodes under his arms as a preventive measure to hopefully stave off the spread of cancer to this area. He was rather reluctant as it was weeks before my wedding to Laurence, after seven years together. Duimpie was adamant that he was going to take part in the preparations and have the joy of walking down the aisle with me. We persuaded him to have the surgery without delay and fortunately the procedure went well. However, he was determined to travel to us at the arranged time and summarily discharged himself earlier than recommended by the oncologist. He knew that it could possibly be his last trip to us. Therefore it meant so much more to him than perhaps any of his previous visits.

Given his pain and discomfort, the long flight from South Africa to England was very uncomfortable to say the least. It was a warm summer that year and he soaked up the joy of being in England once again. He visibly began to relax as the days went on and, although his physical condition was not going to change for the better, psychologically he gained so much from our time together. We spent much time making bows and knick-knacks for our wedding and, when he felt able to do so, he got involved in the various preparations for our big day. On the eve of our wedding, my husband's sons and son-in-law took him out for a stag evening. Duimpie and I, exhausted from all the preparations, opened a bottle of champagne and had a nice, girly evening including all the usual pampering treatments to be expected on the eve of one's wedding. Duimpie could watch my grooming and putting on of make-up for hours as he was fascinated by it all. He would often paint my nails and would do so with the surgical precision and concentration he would have used in the operating theater. Every moment we spent together was precious and in the back of my mind I kept thinking that this might be the last time we would be able to have such private, quality time together.

At the time we lived in a village in the Midlands and diagonally opposite our house was the quintessential English village church. We therefore just had to walk a few yards and cross the road to join our guests for the wedding service. Furthermore, our neighbor lived in the old vicarage with huge gardens and, for the reception we had erected three marquees in her gardens. It truly was an idyllic setting for us as well as our guests. Despite the fact that we could just walk to the church, we played the game of having a friend drive Duimpie and me. After the service my husband and I continued with the pantomime and were driven some distance away for a quiet glass of champagne. The moment we made our way from the car as we returned to our guests, the Royal Air Force display team, the Red Arrows, flew low overhead and Duimpie jokingly shouted, 'It was well worth the £20,000 Laurence paid for the privilege!' To this day many of our guests remain convinced that we had arranged their flypast. However, they were merely on their way to an air display nearby. I don't think, even if we had paid for it, it would have been possible to arrange the timing of their arrival any better.

It was a magical day, not only because it was my wedding, but also it was a lovely English summer's day and all the guests thoroughly enjoyed themselves in the beautiful gardens of our neighbor. To make our wedding even more special was the fact that Duimpie and I made wonderful memories that summer. I have so many photographs, which allow me to relive that memorable and unforgettable summer. Our farewell at the airport was even more emotional than usual. We were intensely grateful for the wonderful time we were able to share while also upset at the thought that we may be saying goodbye for the last time. On his return home, Duimpie and Pieter made the decision to downsize and buy a small town house in a secure complex near the town where they lived. It made it more manageable for Duimpie and it would also be a more suitable place for Pieter when eventually he would be on his own. As it was a secure complex, it also gave Pieter peace of mind in terms of Duimpie's safety when he was at work. However, this was put to the test when shortly after they had moved in

Duimpie had a tumble down the stairs. Fortunately, as well as miraculously, he had no broken bones, just bad bruising. Thankfully, my sister was with him at the time. He would have to learn to navigate stairs more carefully.

He always had his less than graceful moments, particularly when he was in an absent-minded mood, and this was clearly one such occasion. He was known in the family as being the absent-minded professor and could do some very amusing things when his mind was focused on something else, often part of creating a new piece of art. One of his most famous incidents, which was told over and over again in the family, was the time when he had entered a men's clothing shop and engaged a display manikin in a lengthy conversation. It took him some time before he realized that it was a one sided conversation and it was only when the manikin didn't reply that he realized it wasn't a shop assistant! These occasions are what made him so endearing and uniquely Duimpie.

Given that their old house was immaculate and well maintained, it sold very quickly. Once again Duimpie turned his artistic talents to creating a new home for them. Duimpie knew it would be the last home he would create and it therefore became a very special project to him. He spent ages identifying the right position for his various art creations and embroideries and to doing justice to the many pieces of furniture he and Pieter had collected during their years together. Duimpie was always fond of cooking and baking and he was now able to spend many enjoyable hours in the kitchen doing just that. It gave him pleasure to share his culinary creations with Pieter and friends who came around for visits. He also spent considerable time with the resident gardener to create a small but beautiful private area that he could enjoy, either through the patio window from the sitting room or when he was enjoying his afternoon tea on the patio, a ritual he thoroughly relished. He dotted colorful flowers and herbs in tubs around the patio that on a summer's evening mingled to create a unique floral and herbal fragrance. The house and garden were his legacy to Pieter and he wanted them to be a haven for him, a sanctuary where he could find peace and tranquility when eventually Duimpie was no longer with him.

On his next visit to the oncologist Duimpie's PSA markers were showing a significant increase again and the oncologist suggested the next phase of his treatment should be a further course of chemotherapy. Shortly after a number of sessions, Duimpie had to be rushed into hospital with breathing difficulties. Although he had mostly outgrown his childhood lung infections, the chemotherapy had found his weakness. In some cases chemotherapy treatment can affect the lungs, especially if, like Duimpie, the person has a history of lung problems. The drugs had caused inflammation in his lung cells that resulted in an infection known as pneumonitis. Duimpie's doctors also suspected that the drugs had caused the forming of fibrous, scar-like tissues in his lungs, which restricted his lung functioning. The chemotherapy had to cease immediately to prevent any further damage to his fragile lungs. It was a low on the rollercoaster ride for them as they had hoped the chemotherapy would buy them an extra bit of time and possibly help with the quality of Duimpie's life by reducing some of the pain.

They were fast running out of options and the final treatment was radiotherapy. Duimpie had enough medical insight to know they had virtually exhausted the treatment options available to him. Given the fact that he had advanced prostate cancer that had spread to other parts of the body, radiotherapy was merely going to help relieve his symptoms and it would therefore be a palliative treatment rather than any form of cure. The advantage of radiotherapy is that it works relatively quickly and the hope again was that it would help to reduce the pain Duimpie was experiencing and therefore bring some relief to the side effects of the pain medication he was taking. As with the chemotherapy treatment their hope was that it would help to slow down the spread of cancer and give them a bit more time. Duimpie found the radiotherapy treatment the worst of the cocktail of treatments he had had to endure and the pain he suffered shortly after each treatment was intense. He described the sensation as though he had been fried in the areas where the treatment was concentrated. However, in time it did reduce his pain levels and also resulted in a drop of his PSA markers, which was a very good sign.

Duimpie and Pieter tried to live as normal a life as possible given the circumstances and continued to do as many of the things they loved as they could. They had moments of great humor and also moments of intense grief. I suppose to appreciate the humor and laughter one also has to have the opposite. As walking for any length of time became painful to Duimpie they invested in a wheelchair. He was determined to do whatever he could to continue to share a good quality of life with Pieter, and if the use of a wheelchair made that possible, then so be it. It would also be invaluable for a trip they were planning to the Cape Province. Pieter was to spend a month in Cape Town at the offices of the organization he was working for at the time. Duimpie was so excited about the trip as he loved the Cape Province and he and Pieter had often made plans to retire there one day before his diagnosis with cancer. They had made so many memories there and he was very much looking forward to reliving as many of them as possible.

CHAPTER FIFTEEN

To Duimpie and Pieter their pending trip to the Cape Province was akin to that of a pilgrimage as they knew it would be the last time they would visit it together. They had had so many 'last times' over the past five years and this one was particularly special to them. After Duimpie passed away, Pieter also had to get used to the many 'first times' of doing things on his own without Duimpie there to share them. It was also going to be Duimpie's birthday while they were in the Cape and they intended to make it a very special birthday indeed.

The Western Cape is where mountain and sea meet and is one of the most stunning provinces in South Africa, attracting tourists from all over the world. It has majestic mountain ranges with the most famous mountain, of course, being Table Mountain, whose flat top is often shrouded in a white cloud resembling a tablecloth despite it being sunny and warm elsewhere, hence the name. There is a local saying that the Cape is like a baby: it is either wet or windy. Due to its European climate the region produces some of the best wines in the world in valleys nestling at the foot of the mountain ranges. Whenever they came back from a trip to the Western Cape, Duimpie and Pieter would always bring back some of the special wines that aren't widely available in the shops elsewhere and that can only be bought from the local producers. A significant amount of the good wines are exported around the world and the wines produced there have gained popularity, as well as respect, in international wine producing circles.

It is a long journey to the Cape by car from where Duimpie and Pieter lived near Johannesburg and includes a day's travel through the arid, semi-desert of the Karoo plateau. It can be monotonous as the scenery doesn't change much and the main road continues into the distant horizon, virtually in a straight line all the way. The highest mountain peak in the Western Cape, and entrance into the luscious wine valleys, is aptly named Du Toits Kloof Pass (not in our honor, I hasten to add). As soon as the peak becomes visible the traveler knows the end of the day's journey through the desert is in sight. Duimpie used to get so excited when they reached this stage of the journey and, like a child, wanted to know how much further before they got there. Whenever he was excited Duimpie would exclaim enthusiastically, 'I just can NOT wait!' The view that greeted them at this spot always had the power to make them forget their travel weariness. Their ritual was to stop and admire the mountain pass looming before them, which to them resembled the gateway into the city and surrounding countryside they loved so much.

This time the journey took much longer as Duimpie needed more stops on the way to ease the pain and discomfort that resulted from sitting in the car for long stretches at a time. They finally arrived at the apartment they would be staying at for the month and just being immersed in the vibrancy of Cape Town served to lift Duimpie's spirits. Cape Town is also known as the 'Mother City' as it was the first city in South Africa. It is a complex place with a fascinating history. Its diversity is attributed to the mixing of many cultures over the centuries, including slaves from Malaysia, Indonesia, Madagascar, African tribes, the first Dutch settlers and finally the English and French explorers. The mixing of all these cultures has resulted in a vibrant and diverse metropolis with rich cultural attractions. The Malaysian roots have given rise to a style of jazz unique to Cape Town and a street parade known locally as the *Kaapse Klopse* or Minstrel Carnival. It is traditionally held around New Year with hundreds of musicians and dancers adorned in colorful and shiny suits with white painted faces marching through parts of the city, singing and dancing as they go.

Duimpie would venture out for short distances during the days when Pieter was at work and just sit for hours at a café, soaking up the atmosphere, smells, culture and, above all, the uniquely charming lilting accent of the local people. They had a wonderful month, visiting their favorite places such as the spectacular Garden Route and small fishing villages and towns along the coast. They also visited their favorite vineyards to stock up on wine for the trip home. Cape Town is particularly renowned for its exquisite fish restaurants and on Duimpie's birthday they went to their favorite fish restaurant, Bertha's Restaurant in Simon's Town, with a breathtaking view of where the Indian and Atlantic oceans are supposed to meet, watching the sun slowly go down over the sea. When we were kids on holiday in the Cape, Duimpie and I would often be the only ones in this stretch of sea for a number of reasons. Firstly, it was the Cape with its unpredictable weather, secondly because the Atlantic Ocean was much colder than the Indian Ocean. However, we were determined to enjoy a swim in the sea, which we loved to do as kids. On such occasions it would take us at least an hour to thaw out from the cold water, but it was worth every minute.

When it was finally time to go home, they packed up with very heavy, sad hearts and began the slow, long journey home. They followed tradition and stopped at the peak in Du Toits Kloof Pass to have one last look at the rich green valleys below, stretching towards Cape Town in the distance. Words were unnecessary, and would probably be impossible, to convey the depth of their sadness. This would be the last time they would share this view and leaving this spot was excruciatingly painful. As on many occasions before over the years, they were captivated by the majestic beauty of the proud mountains around them, rising up to meet the sky. In folds of green and grey the mountains filled the horizon as far as the eye could see. Peaks rose up from the gentle slopes, and shadows cast by the passing clouds gave some of the peaks a dark and mysterious air.

The beauty of the scenery was made more poignant as they knew they would never again have the opportunity to enjoy it together. The memories came of all the trips to the Cape they had made over the years and the many times they had stopped here, excited for their first glimpse of the Cape, and washed over them in waves. They held tightly onto each other for a very long time, offering a prayer asking for the strength and acceptance for the remainder of the road, both the physical road home as well as their road with cancer. As the light faded and the mountains blended with the darkness of the night sky, they reluctantly tore themselves away from this special place of theirs with all the memories they had associated with it, to continue their long journey home and back to the reality they had been able to escape briefly for a few precious weeks.

Duimpie was beginning to be much more accident-prone and he had a nasty fall shortly after their return from the Cape. He appeared to trip and somehow fell and landed with his knee on his bunch of keys as he was coming through the door. One of the keys cut his knee quite badly and Pieter had to take him to Accident and Emergency, as the cut was deep enough to need a few stitches. Duimpie was also beginning to find it quite difficult and tiring to negotiate the stairs in their home and Pieter, concerned that he might have another fall, created a bedroom for them downstairs. Everything Duimpie needed, including a bathroom, was now on this lower level and it made it much easier for him.

As certain movements such as bending had become difficult and painful he turned to alternative therapies, such as regular pedicures that included reflexology. He also found that aromatherapy and a gentle massage eased the pain, especially in his lower back. This was probably also due to the fact that it helped him to relax. I was rather surprised as he was never one for therapies of this kind, but thankfully he found relief in these methods. Also, the therapist visited Duimpie at home so it meant there was no traveling involved and he could just relax afterwards in his own environment.

What Duimpie and Pieter didn't realize at the time was that the cancer had spread to the bones of the spine, known as a complication called metastatic spinal cord compression (MSCC). The result was that the cancer was pressing on his spinal cord and affecting his movements. Worst case scenario is that it may cause paralysis, preventing normal functioning of the limbs. It is normally accompanied by pain in the arms or legs and weakness in the limbs, making walking and standing difficult. Duimpie had experienced these symptoms for some time now and it was impossible to determine which pain was as a result of the cancer or side effects of the medication. This explained what appeared to be an increase in his natural clumsiness on the occasions when he was being absent-minded. The condition can also affect control of the bladder or bowel movement, but again, this is often a side effect of the many medications of a cancer patient.

Pieter and Duimpie, on one of their regular visits to the oncologist, mentioned these symptoms and he immediately arranged a further scan. The results came back positive for MSCC and he recommended Duimpie have another course of radiotherapy treatment. After his first and very painful experience of radiotherapy, Duimpie decided to think it through and discuss it with Pieter before making a decision. As they were leaving the surgery, the oncologist made a parting comment which to this day I do not know whether to attribute to some form of warped humor or merely a very insensitive throwaway comment. It was at the time of the football World Cup, hosted by South Africa, and the oncologist said that he would have put money on the fact that Duimpie would not have witnessed this event. Duimpie had defied the odds and had lived beyond the maximum five years he was originally given.

In the privacy of their home they went over and over the consequences, possible advantages and inevitable side effects of radiotherapy and the destination to where the road was ultimately and inevitably leading them. Finally, with Pieter's support, Duimpie made the decision that he had had enough of the endless cycle of medications, treatments, scans and side effects and that it was time to let go of the anxieties that surrounded it all.

Having spent nearly 40 years in the medical profession, Duimpie knew the system only too well. As a result of his work one of the benefits he had was a private health scheme to which he made additional monthly contributions. During the 1990s South African private medical aid schemes experienced a significant cost explosion that appeared to be due to very high rates of discretionary, non-lifesaving interventions, such as tonsillectomies, hip replacements for arthritis and so on. Until then, medical schemes tended to simply reimburse the fees submitted by doctors and consultants without either following up whether the interventions were necessary or investigating the cost of such interventions.

Duimpie was always of the opinion that many of the interventions and treatments recommended by the medical teams were either unnecessary or excessive. The commercially driven nature of the private health sector was a constant source of frustration to Duimpie as he saw it as violating the values of care to which he was so committed throughout his career. Patients were treated as cash cows. The response by employers and private health providers to the spiraling costs meant that some organizations abandoned offering medical aid as a benefit of employment or introduced limited benefit packages. Some medical aids also started to determine the health risk of applicants and refused to offer cover to those considered as high risk. Duimpie was very fortunate to have been in his scheme for as long as he was as the costs of his treatment over the five or so years were eye watering. On occasion, Duimpie and Pieter had to pay for some of his treatment as even his generous medical aid had a monthly limit as to the costs it would refund.

Shortly after making his decision Duimpie shared with me that having decided to cease any further treatment felt as though the biggest and heaviest burden had been lifted from his shoulders. For the first time in the five years of living with cancer he could wake up in the morning without the immediate thought that he had to take his first cocktail of drugs before breakfast or his first cup of coffee of the day. He sounded almost elated and went on to describe the relief of waking up from the best night's sleep he had had in many months. Once he had got up, he experienced the sheer joy of just sitting on the patio with a cup of coffee, in the moment, enjoying the flowers and their little private garden without the intrusion of the daily drug regime. The fight of trying to contain the cancer, extending his life for as long as possible, was over. He had finally found a peace to see him through whatever time he had left. I reflected on his words and personally think that, towards the end, much of the fighting to extend his life for as long as possible was mainly for us. He was so aware how difficult it was for all of us to let go of him and, in hindsight, perhaps his own letting go helped us to deal with our own inevitable and eventual loss of him.

Every cancer patient, irrespective of the cancer they have been diagnosed with, will experience their own unique journey. I often reflected on comments in the media when someone famous had passed away as a result of cancer and the reference made to their 'battle with cancer' or their 'fight with cancer'. Having walked with Duimpie on his journey with cancer for nearly six years, I strongly challenge this notion. You don't beat cancer; instead, as Duimpie said, you make friends with it and you embrace it. It is not a competition that has to be won, and with terminal cancer there can only be one winner. His biggest concern right up until the end was for Pieter and who would be there for him; or to put it another way, who wouldn't be there for him?

Coping with terminal cancer is so much more than merely dealing with the physical aspects of the disease. Of equal importance is the psychological pain, frustrations, fears and uncertainties, and in some cases, these are worse. It generated a pain that no amount of morphine could dull. However, making peace with it and, in the words of Mihaly Csikszentmihalyi, learning to go with 'The Flow' leads to the inner harmony Duimpie reached towards the end.

Once again Duimpie found solace in spirituality. He and Pieter discovered a church for the gay community near Johannesburg, which was founded by two gay pastors, Philip and his partner Johan. Duimpie and Philip had many deep discussions about religion, life and, of course, death. Furthermore, the congregation was also a great source of support to both Duimpie and Pieter during the times they were able to attend the services. When it became too difficult for Duimpie to travel, a number of the members of the congregation stayed in touch and visited them at home, as did Philip and Johan whenever they could. Furthermore, they had a significant role to play at the end of Duimpie's life. When faced with the challenges Duimpie and Pieter coped with over their six-year ordeal, the perceived normal interactions with life and rituals of engagement with others are totally rewritten. Significant and meaningful relationships are forged in a short space of time yet with the quality of relationships that have endured many decades.

A key relationship in Duimpie and Pieter's lives, in particular for Pieter, was with Koos and Denise, Pieter's older brother and his wife. From the outset Duimpie had established a strong bond with Denise. Just as Duimpie and I shared a relationship of acceptance of each other, so did Pieter experience the same with his brother and Denise. Throughout the years Duimpie and Pieter were together, they offered them their unconditional acceptance as a couple, including their marriage and everything they represented as a gay couple. Their love and support were invaluable to Duimpie and Pieter during their ordeal with cancer and especially in support of Pieter after Duimpie passed away. Denise, a gifted gardener, had in Duimpie's words created a haven of exotic fauna and flora and he enjoyed spending time among the shades and perfumes offered by the many plants in their garden. Duimpie and Denise had shared many special moments and the two of them would spend hours discussing a wide range of topics from embroidery, knitting and home decorating to, of course, the delights of gardening. During their visits Pieter and his brother Koos would often fade into the background while Duimpie and Denise were engrossed in their discussions.

Duimpie and I had shared so many important and life-changing experiences with each other. I had spent many years studying and researching and Duimpie and Pieter offered constant support to me, sharing the highs and the many lows. I was coming to the end of completing a PhD and I did so in record time. I literally worked seven days a week, in addition to my day-to-day responsibilities as an academic and my various client commitments. I pushed myself as hard as I could and the drive came from the knowledge that Duimpie may not be there to share this final success. I was very lucky to have had a brilliant supervisory team who understood the urgency and my motivations and who gave me all the academic support I needed. Finally, I successfully defended my thesis at the viva and, after phoning my husband to give him the good news, Duimpie was the next person I called. Together we whooped and shouted, and of all the people in my life, he probably had the most insight into what it meant to me. He so desperately wanted to be at my graduation and we talked at length about whether it would be wise and feasible and whether he would have the strength for the long flight. He was adamant that he would be there and, on the same trip, finally visit our place in France. I had my reservations and so did Pieter. However, the decision was ultimately made for us.

I received a very tearful call from Duimpie and it took me some time to understand what he was saying. Finally, the meaning of his words sunk in. He had completely lost the use of his legs and was now paralyzed. I immediately felt guilty at dismissing his increasingly accident-prone behavior as merely Duimpie being his absent-minded self. It all became clear then that the signs had been there for some time and that the paralysis was the result of the metastatic spinal cord compression. It was the inevitable result of the cancer spreading throughout his body. I felt so intensely angry and frustrated with whatever higher power there might be and desperately needed to either assault someone or break the first thing I could lay my hands on.

We had experienced every one of the many possible emotions over the years of Duimpie's illness and sometimes very intensely so. This is a natural part of the journey, but I experienced such a concentration of anger at that moment. Once alone, I screamed and yelled angry accusations at God or whoever one defines as the Ultimate Power. I could not comprehend that the cancer could have made his suffering any worse than that which he had already lived through over the past five or more years, but unbelievably it had. Duimpie was true to his philosophy of life, including his process of dying; if something is worth doing, do it well and with passion.

Thankfully, Pieter had created the bedroom for them downstairs and, with the help of friends and nursing support, they tried to look after Duimpie who now needed virtually 24-hour support. The many day-to-day activities we do without a single thought, such as drinking, washing, brushing our teeth, turning around in bed and so on, now needed conscious planning to enable Duimpie to manage these simple acts for himself. At the same time Duimpie had lost control of his bladder and bowel movements and needed a permanent catheter and pads. They needed so many other tools and utensils merely to carry out normal activities; different cutlery to make eating easier; a special cup to control the flow of liquid so that he didn't choke; and so the list went on.

The big concern Duimpie and Pieter had was the potential of bedsores developing, which are easy to prevent but difficult to treat. As he was unable to turn himself, he had to be manually turned at least every two hours and cream and oil rubbed into the pressure areas on his body. Having stopped all the medication he had lost all the weight gained as a result of the hormone therapy treatment, but as a man of over six feet, it was still a challenge to turn him regularly and not a task easily performed by one person alone. Given his physical condition and his pain levels, it was not possible for him to have periods in a wheelchair and he was therefore completely bed bound.

The toll on Pieter was beginning to show. He was involved in most of Duimpie's daily care, although he had to rely on external help during the day when he had to go to work. Looking after a paralyzed patient is very challenging and demanding as well as being a full time job, without the added burden of a daily job demanding his attention. Duimpie made the very difficult decision that it was going to be impossible for Pieter to cope long term and he couldn't bear to see the visible strain and stress on Pieter, who was trying so desperately to provide him with quality care. Duimpie tasked Pieter to find a nursing home or hospice where he would have the 24-hour nursing support he now needed. With the help of some of Duimpie's colleagues, Pieter found a suitable nursing home that could offer the necessary palliative care.

CHAPTER SIXTEEN

The hospice was located in a quiet suburb of a town near to where Duimpie and Pieter lived and the room Duimpie was allocated was light and airy with big windows and a view over the gardens. It was during times like these that the unbelievable benefit of their marriage was brought home to them. Pieter had to negotiate the care arrangements not only with his medical team and hospice but also with the medical aid provider. He had to wade through reams of forms and doctors' reports to get the final approval before Duimpie could be transferred. Finally, the day came and the ambulance arrived for his transfer to the hospice.

It is impossible to put into words the intensity of emotion and sadness they both experienced. I have described how important Duimpie's home was to him and now he was to be taken away from it, when he needed to be surrounded by the tranquility and harmony they had created over the years. He felt as though a part of him was physically ripped from him and the pain exceeded the most intense pain he had endured from the cancer. He and Pieter held tightly onto each other, crying all the way to the hospice. Once again, and for the last time in his life, Duimpie left his home with only a suitcase. Finally, Duimpie was settled into what would be his final home for whatever time he had left. He was adamant that he didn't want any personal possessions in order to try to create a homely atmosphere. This was a nursing home and he had come here to die. It could never be a home nor replace the home he had left behind.

At least Duimpie was now receiving the nursing care with all the equipment he needed for his physical condition. He had access to advice from various care specialists such as a dietician, physiotherapist and someone experienced in supporting terminally ill patients and their loved ones. Above all, it provided Pieter with the support and respite he desperately needed. Pieter was determined to, where possible, continue to bring normal life into Duimpie's room and on occasions arrived with everything including the kitchen sink! Duimpie received a regular stream of visitors and yet there were those friends who just disappeared. I suppose one can understand why some people would find it too difficult to visit someone who is literally waiting for death. What do you say? What do you talk about? The normal niceties of 'How are you? What have you been up to?' are less appropriate now than ever before.

Duimpie was transferred to the hospice a few weeks before his 60th birthday. When the day arrived my sister Lorenzi adorned the room with balloons and banners and they had a party including birthday cake and 'Happy Birthday' sung by visitors and staff.

Given the age gap, or more like the generation gap, between Lorenzi and Duimpie, it had been difficult for them to forge a close relationship when she was growing up. Her life was taken up with running a business and raising two young children and Duimpie and Pieter led a very different kind of life. However, towards the end they did forge a close relationship and Lorenzi played a key role in maintaining the vigilance during the difficult days at the end of Duimpie's life. It meant a lot to Duimpie to have had that special time with Lorenzi. Throughout it all I stayed in touch with them through FaceTime, telephone calls and videos Pieter regularly sent to me. I was so grateful for the benefit of technology.

Come Christmas Pieter once again decorated Duimpie's room with a Christmas tree, together with all the trimmings, as Duimpie loved Christmas. What do you buy someone who potentially only has weeks, at best months to live? With his usual insight and sensitivity to Duimpie's needs, Pieter bought him a beautiful, leather bound diary in which he regularly wrote and captured the reflections on his life and what it had all meant to him. I arranged my last visit to them following my graduation and went armed with videos and photos of the day and relived the event with Duimpie. We were so grateful that we were able to share this significant event, even if he couldn't be there in person.

Duimpie had lost much of his appetite and his tastes had changed significantly. During my visit Duimpie had a craving for a barbecue and before he had even uttered the words Pieter went home to make all the arrangements and brought the barbecue in the boot of the car, including all the necessary ingredients and equipment to create all his favorite accompanying dishes. As it was summer, the windows and door to Duimpie's room were open and the smells of the barbecue wafted into his room. If it wasn't for the fact that Duimpie was bed bound and with limited time left to live, it felt like any other ordinary family gathering around the barbecue. Looking back, it is fascinating how the human spirit is capable of making the most of what appear to be trivial events in dire circumstances and create a bubble of normality, even if for only a few minutes or hours.

Nothing Duimpie needed was ever too much trouble as far as Pieter was concerned. I was anxious about his own health and mental state and the need for him to somehow be able to replenish his strength and reserves. He would be up at three in the morning, be at Duimpie's bedside when he awoke around 4:30 to wash and shave him and make sure he had his breakfast before he went off to work. He was back again at lunchtime for a visit. After work he would first go to the hospice, supervise Duimpie's evening meal, then only go home to have dinner himself and be back by 8:00 to help Duimpie with his bedtime routine and stay until he fell asleep.

Weekends Pieter would be there during the day and they would watch movies, spend time with visitors or Pieter would sit and work while Duimpie dozed. During each visit Pieter would also massage, with the aid of oils and creams, all the potential areas where Duimpie could possibly develop bedsores. It was his vigilance that meant Duimpie thankfully never developed any such complications. He kept up this relentless pace for the six months Duimpie was in the hospice. Pieter also cajoled and supervised the daily care from the staff, since the levels of care did not match those which Duimpie would have bestowed on his patients. The slide of the standard in nursing care had spilt into all areas of nursing, including hospices such as the one Duimpie was in. I would often reflect in sheer disbelief at the ability of the body to keep going and survive for as long as Duimpie had, despite being consumed by cancer. I felt so guilty for sometimes thinking, please dear God, let go! Don't hang on! What could there possibly be left to live for?

Pieter provided Duimpie with reading material, videos and CDs of his favorite operas and concerts. It became difficult for him to hold a book for any length of time so Pieter brought in a supply of audio books. Although Duimpie and Pieter were mainly classical music lovers, they were particularly fond of a South African singer and actress called Sonja Herholdt. Shortly after Duimpie was transferred to the hospice Sonja was due to release her latest film, a musical called *Liefling* (Darling). Duimpie and Pieter were so disappointed that they would probably not be able to see the movie and were hoping that the DVD would be released in time for them to enjoy it in Duimpie's room. Pieter feared that it was probably going to be too late for Duimpie.

Unbeknown to both of them, their close friend Barry made contact with Sonja, who was so taken with Duimpie's story that, together with the film production company Hartiwood Films, the producer Paul Kruger and his team, she arranged to provide Duimpie and Pieter with a private viewing. They came and set up a big screen in Duimpie's room and Pieter provided all the trimmings one would expect of a trip to the movies, such as popcorn, chocolate, etc. Pieter also took our mother along who was thrilled at meeting the star of the movie. They spent quite some time with Duimpie and Pieter and the opportunity to see the movie and meet Sonja meant a tremendous amount to Duimpie. In fact, Sonja took the time to visit Duimpie on a number of occasions after the private screening. We often perceive famous people as being different human beings from the rest of us, but Sonja and the producer were testimony to the fact that they were ordinary people who were capable of being touched by the trials and tribulations of normal life and of responding with kindness accordingly.

The day-to-day routine of life in the hospice continued for Duimpie and Pieter week after week and then month after month. It was inconceivable just how much one body is able to tolerate before it finally decides it has had enough. Never did any of us, including Duimpie, imagine that he would spend a further six months in a state of suspended animation, waiting for death. I have painted a picture of Duimpie as a very optimistic person with an enormous love of life. It does not mean that he did not have his own very difficult times of depression and deep sadness, because he certainly did. However, his personality always rallied and pulled him through and ensured that the sun would once again break through the dark clouds of pain, loss and anxiety about the unknown. As with so many people before him, he had to come to terms with death and the afterlife, as he perceived it. I often questioned whether it is a blessing or a curse to have the opportunity to do so. For Duimpie and Pieter, their spiritual beliefs were a comfort and helped them to come to terms with the journey and its final destination.

The behavior of Duimpie during his last week or so reflects the experiences others have had with loved ones who are terminally ill. A very sick patient can, all of a sudden for a brief period, make what appears to be a miraculous recovery and this was the case with Duimpie. I will paraphrase the story of his 'comeback' as it was narrated to me by Pieter and Barry. Barry had become a very close friend to both of them and he spent much time with Duimpie during the day, laughing, crying and bitching about life, cancer and the fact that it basically sucks. The story provides a very accurate glimpse into the vibrant personality that once was Duimpie before the cancer took its toll.

The cancer had increasingly affected his co-ordination, leading to involuntary spasms that made simple daily tasks very difficult. However, on Friday the 18th of February, around ten o'clock in the morning, Duimpie surfaced with a bang, as Barry described it. He made a spectacular comeback and, for a brief time, the larger than life personality of Duimpie once again asserted itself. The staff followed the daily routine by giving him his bed bath. However, on this occasion he insisted on shaving himself. He also brushed his teeth without any help and support and the constant involuntary spasms seemed to have subsided. However, Duimpie appeared somewhat confused with different realities overlapping. While engaged in his personal ablutions he asked Barry to hold up his shaving mirror so that he could watch a documentary that was on local television at that time.

This rather strange behavior of watching television in his shaving mirror did not last long and shortly afterwards Duimpie lost interest when the tea lady entered. She offered both Barry and Duimpie some tea, but instead Duimpie said he had a craving for Coca-Cola. This was an unusual request as Duimpie was never partial to the drink and instead preferred coffee. Although puzzled, Barry didn't make much of this request and attributed it, and the request to watch the TV program in his shaving mirror, as a result of the high dosage of morphine Duimpie was on. But Barry soon realized he was wrong and he was encountering a Duimpie that had long ago been subdued.

A couple of days earlier Duimpie insisted during the course of the morning that he had surfaced from a terrible 'fog' and tasked Barry to phone Pieter at work and ask him to bring 'at least six bbbbbiiiiggg Cokes' as he was incredibly thirsty. Without question Pieter obliged and brought him his Cokes as requested. Having consumed most of the drink, on this morning there was only about half a glass left in the last bottle, so Barry obliged and attempted to pour it into a glass for Duimpie. However, Duimpie insisted that the pouring was going to take far too long and drank the Coke directly from the bottle. He was parched! Anyone who knew Duimpie would know that drinking directly out of a bottle was indeed strange behavior, as he certainly deemed it incredibly uncouth for a woman to do so. He took only a few sips and promptly dozed off again. Barry took the bottle from Duimpie and placed it out of sight.

While Duimpie was asleep, Debbie entered Duimpie's room for her regular visit to see how her semi-conscious patient was doing. Or so she thought. Debbie was the nurse assigned to the hospice who offered support and comfort to patients and their families coping with terminal cancer. Duimpie and Pieter referred to her as 'the Angel' as she brought a sense of love and peace into the lives of her patients. To her, supporting terminally ill patients was a vocation and she exuded her commitment in every aspect of her interactions with both the patients and their families alike.

As she walked in, Duimpie opened his eyes and yelled at the top of his voice, 'OOOOOHHH – OOOOHHHH, what wonderful earrings you are wearing!!!!' She was wearing very attractive crystal earrings and their sparkle of rainbow colors clearly captivated Duimpie's attention. To say his sudden reaction gave everyone present a jolt was an understatement. However, years of experience with terminally ill patients meant she effortlessly slipped into her professional role and immediately started chatting with Duimpie as though there was nothing unusual about the conversation. A lot of raucous banter and laughter ensued.

As if picking up an earlier, ongoing conversation, Duimpie started to relay the story about the time when Barry's kindness to support him with his pain management nearly got him arrested by the police at a roadblock. Even though he never got to try the cannabis he was referring to, he started telling Debbie, in what used to be his usual animated and enthusiastic way, how simply WONDERFUL the drug was and that she just HAD to have some. Without further ado, he set about organizing a cannabis tea party. How typical of Duimpie, Barry mused. He so loved to entertain and see everyone happy and having a lovely time. Like a runaway train his enthusiasm gained momentum and he insisted that everyone attending the tea party had to wear hats. However, not any old boring hats, but fancy and flashy ones. He recounted our motto – 'If it's worth doing, darling, it's worth doing in style!' – much to the amusement of those in the room. His insistence on a stylish tea party with fancy hats eventually resulted in the theme for his Life Celebration, an instruction that Pieter carried out after he passed away, but without the cannabis, I hasten to add!

Back to the events of that day. During the discussions and planning of the tea party Duimpie was fully conscious and lucid about what he was saying and doing. Gone was the foggy confusion he expressed earlier when he wanted to watch television in his shaving mirror. For a brief moment, the old Duimpie before cancer took center stage. While the banter and planning of a special tea party continued, Ina, a longtime friend of Duimpie and Pieter, as well as their trusted lawyer, arrived. Once again Duimpie yelled, 'OOOOOOOOOOOOOHHH, let me see that stunning jewelry, doll!' Barry remarked afterwards that he was sure both Ina and Debbie could at that stage have done with some of Duimpie's morphine to help them deal with the shock of suddenly walking in on Duimpie in his animated and exuberant state. This was especially so as their expectations were quite rightly to find him in a semi-conscious state.

Debbie innocently asked Duimpie whether Ina would be joining the tea party, to which Duimpie emphatically responded, 'Absolutely NOT!!! Do you want Ina to have us arrested? She is a lawyer, you know, and I don't think I would now be able to go to jail.' Barry said afterwards that at that point all they could do was to collapse with laughter.

Barry continued with the unfolding of events. By now Duimpie was getting very thirsty from all the talking, laughing and excitement. Duimpie looked around and asked Barry where the last bit of Coke was. Barry picked up the near empty bottle and once again the poor visitors had to hold on to their seats as Duimpie's shouts of joy made everyone jump. If only the sheer delight on his face at the sight of the Coke could have been caught on camera, it would have been an expression Coca-Cola would have been willing to pay any price for, such was his spontaneous joy at the precious liquid. The Coca-Cola slogan at the time was 'Open Happiness' and that was exactly what Coke did for Duimpie, and for a brief instance it opened happiness and joy for him.

Once again Duimpie did what he relished throughout his life, namely to entertain and spread joy and laughter. Pieter was not only stunned, but also delighted to hear Duimpie's voice full of laughter when he phoned to speak to him. Our mother also rang during this time and put the phone down and called back again as she was convinced that she had the wrong number given all the background noise and whoops of laughter. Lunchtime arrived amidst further entertainment. Duimpie teased the poor nurse responsible for bringing his lunch and asked whether she was trying to kill him with 'that food'. He waved the food away and asked her in his most 'flapping dramatic' voice to 'please take that food away immediately, it's poison!' Then he spotted the peach on the tray and once again shouted with joy and insisted that the knife he asked for previously would now come in handy. 'Did I not know earlier in the morning that I was going to be in need of a knife to peel a peach?!' The peach was sliced and diced and with relish he devoured every piece of it.

Duimpie's craving for fruit and yogurt continued and poor Barry was sent to the local supermarket for a long list of various fruits he was longing for. Barry, so delighted to see him enjoying not only the fruit, but also the company of his friends, gladly obliged. Duimpie could not wait for Barry to return and got Ina to phone him twice in the 20 minutes he was gone to determine what was the delay. When Barry returned he was greeted with the comment, 'What took you so long? Are you trying to starve me?!' They continued to joke and laugh and for Barry and the others it was the most precious few hours they had spent with Duimpie for a very long time. It was as though a ghost from the past had come to visit. The room was filled with an atmosphere of happiness and, as Barry commented afterwards, for all of them including Duimpie, there was so much joy and peace and a tangible expression of the adage to live for the moment. That was all that mattered and for a very brief period the pain and illness had indeed been banished from the room.

The weather was not particularly hot, in fact it was quite cool and both Ina and Barry commented on it. Duimpie always preferred the colder weather but being the person he was, he asked Barry if he would go and see if there were some gowns in the linen room for Ina as she was cold. There he was, still taking care of others and not missing even the small discomfort of those around him. It was in his DNA to love and care for others, despite his own pain and discomfort. Barry offered the simple statement that 'Duimpie was made out of Love'. And that probably captured the essence of who he was. By then Duimpie was getting tired and the exuberant merrymaking was taking its toll.

However, he was animated enough to welcome a longstanding friend, Gerrie, later in the afternoon after the earlier visit of Ina. He was a different Gerrie from the one Duimpie and Pieter used to call their 'daughter'. Gerrie was equally surprised to find Duimpie in such good spirits. He tenderly started wiping Duimpie's face only to be told to put some vigor into it. Duimpie and Gerrie started reminiscing about the years of friendship they had shared and relayed to Barry stories from their days around the sewing machine, and of course it was told with melodramatic flare and waving of hands as only Duimpie could do.

Gerrie and his partner Hennie have been together for many years. Hennie was a fashion designer and, among many other designs, he used to make the most exquisite ball gowns for the dancers in Johannesburg. Gerrie was his right hand man and together they would spend time sewing on sequins and beads until the early hours of the morning. I used to love visiting them with Duimpie and would salivate at the sight of the gorgeous gowns and creations Hennie had made. They were such a fun couple and we had many happy memories of times spent with them. Gerrie was equally creative and baked and decorated the most beautiful and unusual cakes. Duimpie and I could guarantee that we would be spoilt with mouthwatering homemade cake when visiting them. With Duimpie's sweet tooth there was not a lot left by the time we bade them farewell.

Barry tried to persuade Duimpie to have a rest before Pieter arrived, as he so wanted Pieter, even for only a brief spell, to enjoy the old Duimpie that had resurfaced. However, under no condition was he going to have a rest. It was much more exciting catching up with friends and doing what he always enjoyed and did best, namely to entertain and engage with people. Pieter arrived just after two o'clock and was delighted to see Duimpie so clearly enjoying the company of their friends. He, of course, remembered to bring Coca-Cola as everyone was doing by then, a sort of entrance fee to see 'Her Majesty' as Barry described him. The final visitor for the afternoon was Barry's sister, Charmaine, and while Pieter and Barry went for something to eat, they had a good chat. Duimpie shared with her that he was ready to go, that he was at peace with God and that all was well. His final comment to her was how much he loved and respected our mother.

Duimpie had an enormous love and zest for life and he was fond of saying, 'Open a new window!', meaning embrace life and whatever new experiences may come your way. If he got enthusiastic or carried away by new adventures he would excitedly say, 'Never mind a window, open a patio door, doll!' His zest for life never waned, despite dark and painful moments during his illness. He was adamant that life and relationships were about 'making memories', as he was so fond of saying.

Barry reflected afterwards that it was impossible to convey in words the experience of that day and the privilege to have had a final glimpse of the Duimpie we had all loved and adored in our own way. As Pieter remarked in a blog he kept for a year after Duimpie passed away, people cross your path and bring support when you need it most. Barry's reflections of that precious day with Duimpie mentioned only a few of the people who supported both Duimpie and Pieter on their long journey with cancer.

Later that afternoon the old Duimpie faded away and he once again drifted in and out of consciousness. Pieter set up a 24-hour vigil with friends and family so that Duimpie would not be on his own. Pieter arranged with the hospice for him to have a bed installed in Duimpie's room so that he could be with him during the night. When he left for work in the morning, dear friends like Barry or my sister would keep vigil until Pieter returned. Pieter was determined that Duimpie was not going to die on his own without a loved one there to hold his hand. I am so grateful that it was with Pieter by his side that he finally drifted away, peacefully, at 6:45 on the evening of the 28th of February, a week after the day he entertained friends with the exuberance only Duimpie was capable of.

All that remains for me to say is, Goodnight Doll.

CONCLUSION

Duimpie was determined that his remembrance service should be a celebration of life, especially the life and love he had had with Pieter. Pieter complied to the letter and the exotic tea party Duimpie had planned on his last day with friends was carried out just as he had wished. Everyone who attended his Life Celebration had to wear silly hats, and what a wonderful sight it was with all their gay friends at their most dramatic and camp, competing to wear the most spectacular and outrageous hat at the service! It created the fun and laughter Duimpie would have wanted and which so aptly captured his nature. I can just imagine how he would have roared with laughter at everyone in their hats, which ranged from the sublime to the ridiculous. The memorial service was held in the hall of the hospice where Duimpie spent the last few months of his life.

Gerrie, their 'daughter', took care of the catering and in tribute he provided some of Duimpie's favorite dishes. A florist friend of Duimpie and Pieter's created a beautiful display with all the flowers Duimpie loved and which remained at the hospice afterwards. It was fitting that Trevor, Gerrie's partner and the Minister who had married Duimpie and Pieter, would be one of the people to lead his Life Celebration service. The other person with whom Trevor shared the conducting of the proceedings was Philip, the pastor and co-founder of the gay church who had offered so much support to Duimpie and Pieter in the latter stages of their journey. Philip started off the proceedings, representing the lighter and fun loving side of Duimpie, while Trevor concluded the service in a more traditional and reflective tone. Together they led the final goodbyes to an exceptional human being who had touched so many people with so much love throughout his life.

Shortly after the Life Celebration for Duimpie, he was cremated and a few weeks later, Pieter and I, together with their dear friend Barry, went on a pilgrimage to Clarens for the scattering of his ashes. It was Duimpie's wish that his ashes be scattered on the spot where he and Pieter were married. Pieter often returns to Clarens for his private pilgrimage, in particular on the 1st of December every year, which is the anniversary of their wedding day. We spent a few days in Clarens, visiting all their favorite places. It was a cathartic few days that allowed us to talk, cry, laugh and remember together.

Finally, with the near six-year ordeal behind him, Pieter could grieve and mourn the passing of his love and begin another long journey of learning to live life without Duimpie by his side. Pieter described the depth of his own suffering resulting from observing Duimpie's suffering over the years, as both physical and emotional trauma and bruising. The trauma of the six years on the rollercoaster ride with Duimpie stayed with Pieter for a long time and, as with physical bruising, the deeper bruises took time to surface, change color and eventually fade. Step by step he began to adjust to life without Duimpie and he went through a phase where he felt almost guilty to even think of doing things on his own without Duimpie by his side. He and Duimpie spent every available minute with each other and they would not think of planning anything without consulting the other one first. It is hard to discard behavior patterns and, as Pieter said, it was about reprograming the mind and putting new routines and structures in place; routines that did not include Duimpie.

Despite all the previously mentioned positive angles, as Pieter reflected, the sadness of losing a loved one remains overwhelming and the awareness of the gaps that are left by their physical absence become more prominent as time passes. The first significant gap Pieter had experienced was in 1973 when his father passed away when he was only 13 years old. At the age of 56, when Pieter put together all the gaps that had formed in his life, following the loss of a number of his loved ones, they combined to become a massive gaping hole; a dark hole sometimes so intimidating and powerful that it threatened to swallow up his whole universe. No matter how many good memories one has of a loved one who has passed away, or how frequently one still engages in 'conversations' with them, nothing helps to close that massive gaping hole. Only time has the capacity to do so.

For a very long time after the death of a loved one, the surviving partner is often taken by surprise when an inconsequential event or experience can trigger a flood of emotion and a sense of loss. Pieter shared one such moment when one afternoon, having done some gardening, the radio played a favorite song of his and Duimpie's while he was sitting with a cup of coffee looking out at the garden. Out of nowhere, on hearing that song, he was overwhelmed with intense sadness not knowing where Duimpie really was. For the first time he felt totally 'rattled' in his words by not knowing EXACTLY (as in GPS coordinates, exact location) where Duimpie was. The 'somewhereness' of the hereafter suddenly hit him and he felt quite derailed. Looking around at his surroundings, the house and everything within it which he and Duimpie had spent years building up, it all suddenly felt so intensely empty without him physically by his side.

Each one of us has our own strategies that help us to cope and come to terms with the loss of those we love. For Pieter, one of his strategies was to clear out their cupboards. Duimpie had a passion for sorting out cupboards and keeping things in order. As I said, our mother always chastised me for not being as tidy as Duimpie was. He was of the opinion that not only did the physical act of clearing out the cupboards make room for new things, but that it was also true of emotional hoarding and attachments. He had learnt earlier in his life the value of letting go of various attachments. However, this meant that Pieter was therefore never involved in the sorting out of the cupboards and whenever he was looking for something, he would simply ask Duimpie in which cupboard it could be found. As Duimpie deteriorated, his 'cupboard sessions' became fewer and fewer.

After he had passed away, Pieter had almost a sense of 'disconnection' with the contents of the cupboards. He had some idea where the most important things were, but there were a number of cupboards whose contents were a total mystery to him. He spent several weeks systematically working through all the cupboards to rearrange and sort out the contents. Going through everything brought back a flood of memories and he was once again reminded by his discoveries what a truly rich and fulfilled life they had together. It was both an emotional experience sorting through everything, but it was also a celebration of their years together.

Pieter has continued to be the pillar of strength in our family. When our mother was taken into a nursing home suffering from dementia it was Pieter who provided the strength and support to my sister with the necessary arrangements for her care. It was once again Pieter who was there to provide our mother with his boundless care and support and hold her hand when she finally passed away. It was Pieter who scattered our mother's ashes in the same spot in Clarens where we had previously scattered Duimpie's.

It is the indistinguishable flame of love for life that Duimpie had which was one of my motivations for writing this book. Like our mother, he had the ability to find the positive in any situation after he picked himself up and accepted whatever life had put in his path. Ever since I can remember, I had a feeling that there was something very specific I had to do in this life, yet that purpose kept eluding me. I often shared this feeling with Duimpie. I have come to the belief that writing this tribute to Duimpie and Pieter, their exceptional love that sustained them through an unimaginably difficult journey and the depth of love and support Pieter gave Duimpie is what I came here to do. I am so privileged to have so many memories of our times together, a few of which I have shared with you in this tribute. I reach out to every one of you, patient, friend or family of a cancer patient and carers, and I hope that this tribute will offer some support and comfort to you on your own journey.

I have kept a blog, entitled *One Step at a Time*, for a year or so while writing this tribute to Duimpie and Pieter. Its purpose was to reflect on the actual process of writing this tribute and the many challenges I encountered as part of the journey, both of a practical nature as well as an emotional one. It is available at https://angelontheroof.wordpress.com and also features many of the photographs that accompany the experiences and stories I have shared in the book, including photos of some of the exotic and bizarre hats worn by everyone who attended Duimpie's Life Celebration service.

Finally, I summarize Duimpie and Pieter's love with the words of the song entitled 'The Wind Beneath My Wings' by Jeff Silbar and Larry Henley that so aptly describes the nature of the relationship they had shared. As the lyrics suggest, Pieter was only too happy for Duimpie to shine, and actively encouraged it, preferring to be in the background, but Pieter provided the strength for him to do so. Pieter truly was Duimpie's hero and Duimpie never grew tired of saying so. Pieter's quiet strength and support allowed Duimpie to soar and eventually face the ultimate challenge and the unimaginably difficult six-year journey of coping with terminal cancer. The final lyrics of the song summarize Duimpie's mantra that he so often uttered, especially during his final years: *'Thank you, thank you, thank God for you (Pieter), the wind beneath my wings.'*

ABOUT THE AUTHOR

Angélique du Toit put on hold a career as an academic and international executive coach in order to write this tribute to her gay brother and his partner. She has made a significant contribution to the development of organizational leadership through research and the publication of a number of books on the subject. Other books published by her include *Corporate Strategy: A Feminist Perspective*, followed by *Rethinking Coaching: Critical Theory and the Economic Crisis*, and recently *Making Sense of Coaching*. Her time is spent in the East Midlands and the North East of England as well as the South of France.

If you have enjoyed or benefitted from her book please take a few minutes to write a review on Amazon to help raise awareness of cancer and prostate cancer in particular. Even if it's only a line or two, it would be a *huge* help.

If you want to get an automatic email when Angélique's next book is released, sign up here http://eepurl.com/bMSdCT You will only be contacted when a new book is released, your address will never be shared and you can unsubscribe at any time.

Printed in Great Britain
by Amazon.co.uk, Ltd.,
Marston Gate.